Also by Ted Hughes

Selected Poems

1957–1994

TED HUGHES

Selected Poems

1957–1994

FARRAR, STRAUS AND GIROUX

NEW YORK

FARRAR, STRAUS AND GIROUX
19 Union Square West, New York 10003

Copyright © 1995, 2002 by The Estate of Ted Hughes
Printed in the United States of America
Originally published in 1995 by Faber and Faber Ltd, Great Britain,
as *New Selected Poems 1957–1994*
Published in the United States by Farrar, Straus and Giroux
First American edition, 2002

Library of Congress Cataloging-in-Publication Data
Hughes, Ted, 1930–
    [Poems. Selections]
    Selected poems, 1957–1994 / Ted Hughes.— 1st Farrar, Straus and
Giroux ed.
        p. cm.
    ISBN 0-374-25875-9 (alk. paper) — ISBN 0-374-52864-0 (pbk. : alk. paper)
    I. Title.

PR6058.U37 A6 2002b
821'.914—dc21

                                                        2002021603

www.fsgbooks.com

1   3   5   7   9   10   8   6   4   2

CONTENTS

from CAVE BIRDS (1975)

from RAIN-CHARM FOR THE DUCHY (1992)

xiii

Selected Poems

1957–1994

The Thought-Fox

I imagine this midnight moment's forest:
Something else is alive
Beside the clock's loneliness
And this blank page where my fingers move.

Through the window I see no star:
Something more near
Though deeper within darkness
Is entering the loneliness:

Cold, delicately as the dark snow
A fox's nose touches twig, leaf;
Two eyes serve a movement, that now
And again now, and now, and now

Sets neat prints into the snow
Between trees, and warily a lame
Shadow lags by stump and in hollow
Of a body that is bold to come

Across clearings, an eye,
A widening deepening greenness,
Brilliantly, concentratedly,
Coming about its own business

Till, with a sudden sharp hot stink of fox
It enters the dark hole of the head.
The window is starless still; the clock ticks,
The page is printed.

Song

O lady, when the tipped cup of the moon blessed you
You became soft fire with a cloud's grace;
The difficult stars swam for eyes in your face;
You stood, and your shadow was my place:
You turned, your shadow turned to ice
    O my lady.

O lady, when the sea caressed you
You were a marble of foam, but dumb.
When will the stone open its tomb?
When will the waves give over their foam?
You will not die, nor come home,
    O my lady.

O lady, when the wind kissed you
You made him music for you were a shaped shell.
I follow the waters and the wind still
Since my heart heard it and all to pieces fell
Which your lovers stole, meaning ill,
    O my lady.

O lady, consider when I shall have lost you
The moon's full hands, scattering waste,
The sea's hands, dark from the world's breast,
The world's decay where the wind's hands have passed,
And my head, worn out with love, at rest
In my hands, and my hands full of dust,
    O my lady.

The Jaguar

The apes yawn and adore their fleas in the sun.
The parrots shriek as if they were on fire, or strut
Like cheap tarts to attract the stroller with the nut.
Fatigued with indolence, tiger and lion

Lie still as the sun. The boa-constrictor's coil
Is a fossil. Cage after cage seems empty, or
Stinks of sleepers from the breathing straw.
It might be painted on a nursery wall.

But who runs like the rest past these arrives
At a cage where the crowd stands, stares, mesmerized,
As a child at a dream, at a jaguar hurrying enraged
Through prison darkness after the drills of his eyes

On a short fierce fuse. Not in boredom –
The eye satisfied to be blind in fire,
By the bang of blood in the brain deaf the ear –
He spins from the bars, but there's no cage to him

More than to the visionary his cell:
His stride is wildernesses of freedom:
The world rolls under the long thrust of his heel.
Over the cage floor the horizons come.

Famous Poet

Stare at the monster: remark
How difficult it is to define just what
Amounts to monstrosity in that
Very ordinary appearance. Neither thin nor fat,
    Hair between light and dark,

    And the general air
Of an apprentice – say, an apprentice house-
Painter amid an assembly of famous
Architects: the demeanour is of mouse,
    Yet is he monster.

    First scrutinize those eyes
For the spark, the effulgence: nothing. Nothing there
But the haggard stony exhaustion of a near-

Finished variety artist. He slumps in his chair
Like a badly hurt man, half life-size.

Is it his dreg-boozed inner demon
Still tankarding from tissue and follicle
The vital fire, the spirit electrical
That puts the gloss on a normal hearty male?
Or is it women?

The truth – bring it on
With black drapery, drums and funeral tread
Like a great man's coffin – no, no, he is not dead
But in this truth surely half-buried:
Once, the humiliation

Of youth and obscurity,
The autoclave of heady ambition trapped,
The fermenting of the yeasty heart stopped –
Burst with such pyrotechnics the dull world gaped
And 'Repeat that!' still they cry.

But all his efforts to concoct
The old heroic bang from their money and praise
From the parent's pointing finger and the child's amaze,
Even from the burning of his wreathed bays,
Have left him wrecked: wrecked,

And monstrous, so,
As a Stegosaurus, a lumbering obsolete
Arsenal of gigantic horn and plate
From a time when half the world still burned, set
To blink behind bars at the zoo.

Soliloquy

Whenever I am got under my gravestone
Sending my flowers up to stare at the church-tower,
Gritting my teeth in the chill from the church-floor,
I shall praise God heartily, to see gone,

As I look round at old acquaintance there,
Complacency from the smirk of every man,
And every attitude showing its bone,
And every mouth confessing its crude shire;

But I shall thank God thrice heartily
To be lying beside women who grimace
Under the commitments of their flesh,
And not out of spite or vanity.

The Horses

I climbed through woods in the hour-before-dawn dark.
Evil air, a frost-making stillness,

Not a leaf, not a bird, –
A world cast in frost. I came out above the wood

Where my breath left tortuous statues in the iron light.
But the valleys were draining the darkness

Till the moorline – blackening dregs of the brightening
    grey –
Halved the sky ahead. And I saw the horses:

Huge in the dense grey – ten together –
Megalith-still. They breathed, making no move,

With draped manes and tilted hind-hooves,
Making no sound.

I passed: not one snorted or jerked its head.
Grey silent fragments

Of a grey silent world.

I listened in emptiness on the moor-ridge.
The curlew's tear turned its edge on the silence.

Slowly detail leafed from the darkness. Then the sun
Orange, red, red erupted.

Silently, and splitting to its core tore and flung cloud,
Shook the gulf open, showed blue,

And the big planets hanging –
I turned

Stumbling in the fever of a dream, down towards
The dark woods, from the kindling tops,

And came to the horses.
                    There, still they stood,
But now steaming and glistening under the flow of light,

Their draped stone manes, their tilted hind-hooves
Stirring under a thaw while all around them

The frost showed its fires. But still they made no sound.
Not one snorted or stamped,

Their hung heads patient as the horizons
High over valleys, in the red levelling rays –

In din of the crowded streets, going among the years, the
    faces,
May I still meet my memory in so lonely a place

Between the streams and the red clouds, hearing
    curlews,
Hearing the horizons endure.

Fallgrief's Girlfriends

Not that she had no equal, not that she was
His before flesh was his or the world was;
Not that she had the especial excellence
To make her cat-indolence and shrew-mouth
Index to its humanity. Her looks
Were what a good friend would not comment on.
If he made flattery too particular,
Admiring her cookery or lipstick,
Her eyes reflected painfully. Yet not that
He pitied her: he did not pity her.

'Any woman born,' he said, 'having
What any woman born cannot but have,
Has as much of the world as is worth more
Than wit or lucky looks can make worth more;
And I, having what I have as a man
Got without choice, and what I have chosen,
City and neighbour and work, am poor enough
To be more than bettered by a worst woman.
Whilst I am this muck of man in this
Muck of existence, I shall not seek more
Than a muck of a woman: wit and lucky looks
Were a ring disabling this pig-snout,
And a tin clasp on this diamond.'

By this he meant to break out of the dream
Where admiration's giddy mannequin
Leads every sense to motley; he meant to stand naked
Awake in the pitch dark where the animal runs,
Where the insects couple as they murder each other,
Where the fish outwait the water.
                              The chance changed him:
He has found a woman of such wit and looks
He can brag of her in every company.

Egg-Head

A leaf's otherness,
The whaled monstered sea-bottom, eagled peaks
And stars that hang over hurtling endlessness,
    With manslaughtering shocks

Are let in on his sense:
So many a one has dared to be struck dead
Peeping through his fingers at the world's ends,
    Or at an ant's head.

But better defence
Than any militant pride are the freebooting crass
Veterans of survival and those champions
    Forgetfulness, madness.

Brain in deft opacities,
Walled in translucencies, shuts out the world's knocking
With a welcome, and to wide-eyed deafnesses
    Of prudence lets it speak.

Long the eggshell head's
Fragility rounds and resists receiving the flash
Of the sun, the bolt of the earth: and feeds
    On the yolk's dark and hush

Of a helplessness coming
By feats of torpor, by circumventing sleights
Of stupefaction, juggleries of benumbing,
    By lucid sophistries of sight

To a staturing 'I am',
To the upthrust affirmative head of a man.
Braggart-browed complacency in most calm
    Collusion with his own

Dewdrop frailty
Must stop the looming mouth of the earth with a pin-
Point cipher, with a blank-stare courtesy
    Confront it and preen,

    Spurn it muck under
His foot-clutch, and, opposing his eye's flea-red
Fly-catching fervency to the whelm of the sun,
    Trumpet his own ear dead.

Vampire

You hosts are almost glad he gate-crashed: see,
How his eyes brighten on the whisky, how his wit
Tumbles the company like a lightning stroke –
You marvel where he gets his energy from . . .

But that same instant, here, far underground,
This fusty carcase stirs its shroud and swells.

'Stop, stop, oh for God's sake, stop!' you shriek
As your tears run down, but he goes on and on
Mercilessly till you think your ribs must crack . . .

While this carcase's eyes grimace, stitched
In the cramp of an ordeal, and a squeeze of blood
Crawls like scorpions into its hair.

You plead, limp, dangling in his mad voice, till
With a sudden blood-spittling cough, he chokes: he
    leaves
Trembling, soon after. You slump back down in a chair
Cold as a leaf, your heart scarcely moving . . .

Deep under the city's deepest stone
This grinning sack is bursting with your blood.

The Man Seeking Experience Enquires His Way of a Drop of Water

'This water droplet, charity of the air,
Out of the watched blue immensity –
(Where, where are the angels?) out of the draught in the
  door,
The Tuscarora, the cloud, the cup of tea,
The sweating victor and the decaying dead bird –
This droplet has travelled far and studied hard.

'Now clings on the cream paint of our kitchen wall.
Aged eye! This without heart-head-nerve lens
Which saw the first and earth-centering jewel
Spark upon darkness, behemoth bulk and lumber
Out of the instant flash, and man's hand
Hoist him upright, still hangs clear and round.

'Having studied a journey in the high
Cathedralled brain, the mole's ear, the fish's ice,
The abattoir of the tiger's artery,
The slum of the dog's bowel, and there is no place
His bright look has not bettered, and problem none
But he has brought it to solution.

'Venerable elder! Let us learn of you.
Read us a lesson, a plain lesson how
Experience has worn or made you anew,
That on this humble kitchen wall hang now,
O dew that condensed of the breath of the Word
On the mirror of the syllable of the Word.'

So he spoke, aloud, grandly, then stood
For an answer, knowing his own nature all
Droplet-kin, sisters and brothers of lymph and blood,
Listened for himself to speak for the drop's self.
This droplet was clear simple water still.
It no more responded than the hour-old child

Does to finger-toy or coy baby-talk,
But who lies long, long and frowningly
Unconscious under the shock of its own quick
After that first alone-in-creation cry
When into the mesh of sense, out of the dark,
Blundered the world-shouldering monstrous 'I'.

Meeting

He smiles in a mirror, shrinking the whole
Sun-swung zodiac of light to a trinket shape
    On the rise of his eye: it is a role

In which he can fling a cape,
And outloom life like Faustus. But once when
    On an empty mountain slope

A black goat clattered and ran
Towards him, and set forefeet firm on a rock
    Above and looked down

A square-pupilled yellow-eyed look
The black devil head against the blue air,
    What gigantic fingers took

Him up and on a bare
Palm turned him close under an eye
    That was like a living hanging hemisphere

And watched his blood's gleam with a ray
Slow and cold and ferocious as a star
    Till the goat clattered away.

Wind

This house has been far out at sea all night,
The woods crashing through darkness, the booming
 hills,
Winds stampeding the fields under the window
Floundering black astride and blinding wet

Till day rose; then under an orange sky
The hills had new places, and wind wielded
Blade-light, luminous black and emerald,
Flexing like the lens of a mad eye.

At noon I scaled along the house-side as far as
The coal-house door. Once I looked up –
Through the brunt wind that dented the balls of my eyes
The tent of the hills drummed and strained its guyrope,

The fields quivering, the skyline a grimace,
At any second to bang and vanish with a flap:
The wind flung a magpie away and a black-
Back gull bent like an iron bar slowly. The house

Rang like some fine green goblet in the note
That any second would shatter it. Now deep
In chairs, in front of the great fire, we grip
Our hearts and cannot entertain book, thought,

Or each other. We watch the fire blazing,
And feel the roots of the house move, but sit on,
Seeing the window tremble to come in,
Hearing the stones cry out under the horizons.

October Dawn

October is marigold, and yet
A glass half full of wine left out

To the dark heaven all night, by dawn
Has dreamed a premonition

Of ice across its eye as if
The ice-age had begun its heave.

The lawn overtrodden and strewn
From the night before, and the whistling green

Shrubbery are doomed. Ice
Has got its spearhead into place.

First a skin, delicately here
Restraining a ripple from the air;

Soon plate and rivet on pond and brook;
Then tons of chain and massive lock

To hold rivers. Then, sound by sight
Will Mammoth and Sabre-tooth celebrate

Reunion while a fist of cold
Squeezes the fire at the core of the world,

Squeezes the fire at the core of the heart,
And now it is about to start.

The Casualty

Farmers in the fields, housewives behind steamed
    windows,
Watch the burning aircraft across the blue sky float,
As if a firefly and a spider fought,
Far above the trees, between the washing hung out.
They wait with interest for the evening news.

But already, in a brambled ditch, suddenly-smashed
Stems twitch. In the stubble a pheasant
Is craning every way in astonishment.

The hare that hops up, quizzical, hesitant,
Flattens ears and tears madly away and the wren warns.

Some, who saw fall, smoke beckons. They jostle above,
They peer down a sunbeam as if they expected there
A snake in the gloom of the brambles or a rare flower –
See the grave of dead leaves heave suddenly, hear
It was a man fell out of the air alive,

Hear now his groans and senses groping. They rip
The slum of weeds, leaves, barbed coils; they raise
A body that as the breeze touches it glows,
Branding their hands on his bones. Now that he has
No spine, against heaped sheaves they prop him up,

Arrange his limbs in order, open his eye,
Then stand, helpless as ghosts. In a scene
Melting in the August noon, the burned man
Bulks closer greater flesh and blood than their own,
As suddenly the heart's beat shakes his body and the eye

Widens childishly. Sympathies
Fasten to the blood like flies. Here's no heart's more
Open or large than a fist clenched, and in there
Holding close complacency its most dear
Unscratchable diamond. The tears of their eyes

Too tender to let break, start to the edge
Of such horror close as mourners can,
Greedy to share all that is undergone,
Grimace, gasp, gesture of death. Till they look down
On the handkerchief at which his eye stares up.

Bayonet Charge

Suddenly he awoke and was running – raw
In raw-seamed hot khaki, his sweat heavy,
Stumbling across a field of clods towards a green hedge

That dazzled with rifle fire, hearing
Bullets smacking the belly out of the air –
He lugged a rifle numb as a smashed arm;
The patriotic tear that had brimmed in his eye
Sweating like molten iron from the centre of his chest –

In bewilderment then he almost stopped –
In what cold clockwork of the stars and the nations
Was he the hand pointing that second? He was running
Like a man who has jumped up in the dark and runs
Listening between his footfalls for the reason
Of his still running, and his foot hung like
Statuary in mid-stride. Then the shot-slashed furrows

Threw up a yellow hare that rolled like a flame
And crawled in a threshing circle, its mouth wide
Open silent, its eyes standing out.
He plunged past with his bayonet towards the green
    hedge,
King, honour, human dignity, etcetera
Dropped like luxuries in a yelling alarm
To get out of that blue crackling air
His terror's touchy dynamite.

Six Young Men

The celluloid of a photograph holds them well –
Six young men, familiar to their friends.
Four decades that have faded and ochre-tinged
This photograph have not wrinkled the faces or the
    hands.
Though their cocked hats are not now fashionable,
Their shoes shine. One imparts an intimate smile,
One chews a grass, one lowers his eyes, bashful,
One is ridiculous with cocky pride –
Six months after this picture they were all dead.

All are trimmed for a Sunday jaunt. I know
That bilberried bank, that thick tree, that black wall,
Which are there yet and not changed. From where these
    sit
You hear the water of seven streams fall
To the roarer in the bottom, and through all
The leafy valley a rumouring of air go.
Pictured here, their expressions listen yet,
And still that valley has not changed its sound
Though their faces are four decades under the ground.

This one was shot in an attack and lay
Calling in the wire, then this one, his best friend,
Went out to bring him in and was shot too;
And this one, the very moment he was warned
From potting at tin-cans in no man's land,
Fell back dead with his rifle-sights shot away.
The rest, nobody knows what they came to,
But come to the worst they must have done, and held it
Closer than their hope; all were killed.

Here see a man's photograph,
The locket of a smile, turned overnight
Into the hospital of his mangled last
Agony and hours; see bundled in it
His mightier-than-a-man dead bulk and weight:
And on this one place which keeps him alive
(In his Sunday best) see fall war's worst
Thinkable flash and rending, onto his smile
Forty years rotting into soil.

That man's not more alive whom you confront
And shake by the hand, see hale, hear speak loud,
Than any of these six celluloid smiles are,
Nor prehistoric or fabulous beast more dead;
No thought so vivid as their smoking-blood:
To regard this photograph might well dement,

Such contradictory permanent horrors here
Smile from the single exposure and shoulder out
One's own body from its instant and heat.

The Martyrdom of Bishop Farrar

Burned by Bloody Mary's men at Carmarthen. 'If I flinch from the
pain of the burning, believe not the doctrine that I have preached.'
(His words on being chained to the stake.)

Bloody Mary's venomous flames can curl:
They can shrivel sinew and char bone
Of foot, ankle, knee, and thigh, and boil
Bowels, and drop his heart a cinder down;
And her soldiers can cry, as they hurl
Logs in the red rush: 'This is her sermon.'

The sullen-jowled watching Welsh townspeople
Hear him crack in the fire's mouth; they see what
Black oozing twist of stuff bubbles the smell
That tars and retches their lungs: no pulpit
Of his ever held their eyes so still,
Never, as now his agony, his wit.

An ignorant means to establish ownership
Of his flock! Thus their shepherd she seized
And knotted him into this blazing shape
In their eyes, as if such could have cauterized
The trust they turned towards him, and branded on
Its stump her claim, to outlaw question.

So it might have been: seeing their exemplar
And teacher burned for his lessons to black bits,
Their silence might have disowned him to her,
And hung up what he had taught with their Welsh hats:
Who sees his blasphemous father struck by fire
From heaven, might well be heard to speak no oaths.

But the fire that struck here, come from Hell even,
Kindled little heavens in his words
As he fed his body to the flame alive.
Words which, before they will be dumbly spared,
Will burn their body and be tongued with fire
Make paltry folly of flesh and this world's air.

When they saw what annuities of hours
And comfortable blood he burned to get
His words a bare honouring in their ears,
The shrewd townsfolk pocketed them hot:
Stamp was not current but they rang and shone
As good gold as any queen's crown.

Gave all he had, and yet the bargain struck
To a merest farthing his whole agony,
His body's cold-kept miserdom of shrieks
He gave uncounted, while out of his eyes,
Out of his mouth, fire like a glory broke,
And smoke burned his sermon into the skies.

Song from Bawdry Embraced

From what dog's dish or crocodile's rotten
    Larder she had come
He questioned none: 'It is enough
    That she is and I am.'

They caught each other by the body
    And fell in a heap:
A cockerel there struck up a tread
    Like a cabman's whip.

And so they knit, knotted and wrought
    Braiding their ends in;
So fed their radiance to themselves
    They could not be seen.

And thereupon – a miracle!
    Each became, a lens
So focussing creation's heat
    The other burst in flames.

Bawdry! Bawdry! Steadfastly
    Thy great protagonists
Died face to face, with bellies full,
    In the solar waste

Where there is neither skirt nor coat,
    And every ogling eye
Is a cold star to measure
    Their solitude by.

Mayday on Holderness

This evening, motherly summer moves in the pond.
I look down into the decomposition of leaves –
The furnace door whirling with larvae.

From Hull's sunset smudge
Humber is melting eastward, my south skyline:
A loaded single vein, it drains
The effort of the inert North – Sheffield's ores.
Bog pools, dregs of toadstools, tributary
Graves, dunghills, kitchens, hospitals.
The unkillable North Sea swallows it all.
Insects, drunken, drop out of the air.

Birth-soils,
The sea-salts, scoured me, cortex and intestine,
To receive these remains.
As the incinerator, as the sun,
As the spider, I had a whole world in my hands.
Flowerlike, I loved nothing.
Dead and unborn are in God comfortable.
What a length of gut is growing and breathing –
This mute eater, biting through the mind's
Nursery floor, with eel and hyena and vulture,
With creepy-crawly and the root,
With the sea-worm, entering its birthright.

The stars make pietas. The owl announces its sanity.

The crow sleeps glutted and the stoat begins.
There are eye-guarded eggs in these hedgerows,
Hot haynests under the roots in burrows.
Couples at their pursuits are laughing in the lanes.

The North Sea lies soundless. Beneath it
Smoulder the wars: to heart-beats, bomb, bayonet.
'Mother, Mother!' cries the pierced helmet.
Cordite oozings of Gallipoli,

Curded to beastings, broached my palate,
The expressionless gaze of the leopard,
The coils of the sleeping anaconda,
The nightlong frenzy of shrews.

February

The wolf with its belly stitched full of big pebbles;
Nibelung wolves barbed like black pineforest
Against a red sky, over blue snow; or that long grin
Above the tucked coverlet – none suffice.

A photograph: the hairless, knuckled feet
Of the last wolf killed in Britain spoiled him for wolves:
The worst since has been so much mere Alsatian.
Now it is the dream cries 'Wolf!' where these feet

Print the moonlit doorstep, or run and run
Through the hush of parkland, bodiless, headless;
With small seeming of inconvenience
By day, too, pursue, siege all thought;

Bring him to an abrupt poring stop
Over engravings of gibbet-hung wolves,
As at a cage where the scraggy Spanish wolf
Danced, smiling, brown eyes doggily begging

A ball to be thrown. These feet, deprived,
Disdaining all that are caged, or storied, or pictured,
Through and throughout the true world search
For their vanished head, for the world

Vanished with the head, the teeth, the quick eyes –
Now, lest they choose his head,
Under severe moons he sits making
Wolf-masks, mouths clamped well onto the world.

Crow Hill

The farms are oozing craters in
Sheer sides under the sodden moors:
When it is not wind it is rain,
Neither of which will stop at doors:
One will damp beds and the other shake
Dreams beneath sleep it cannot break.

Between the weather and the rock
Farmers make a little heat;
Cows that sway a bony back,
Pigs upon delicate feet
Hold off the sky, trample the strength
That shall level these hills at length.

Buttoned from the blowing mist
Walk the ridges of ruined stone.
What humbles these hills has raised
The arrogance of blood and bone,
And thrown the hawk upon the wind,
And lit the fox in the dripping ground.

A Woman Unconscious

Russia and America circle each other;
Threats nudge an act that were without doubt
A melting of the mould in the mother,
Stones melting about the root,

The quick of the earth burned out:
The toil of all our ages a loss
With leaf and insect. Yet flitting thought
(Not to be thought ridiculous)

Shies from the world-cancelling black
Of its playing shadow: it has learned
That there's no trusting (trusting to luck)
Dates when the world's due to be burned;

That the future's no calamitous change
But a malingering of now,
Histories, towns, faces that no
Malice or accident much derange.

And though bomb be matched against bomb,
Though all mankind wince out and nothing endure –
Earth gone in an instant flare –
Did a lesser death come

Onto the white hospital bed
Where one, numb beyond her last of sense,
Closed her eyes on the world's evidence
And into pillows sunk her head?

Strawberry Hill

A stoat danced on the lawns here
To the music of the maskers;
Drinking the staring hare dry, bit
Through grammar and corset. They nailed to a door

The stoat with the sun in its belly,
But its red unmanageable life
Has licked the stylist out of their skulls
Has sucked that age like an egg and gone off

Along ditches where flies and leaves
Overpower our tongues, got into some grave –
Not a dog to follow it down –
Emerges, thirsting, in far Asia, in Brixton.

Fourth of July

The hot shallows and seas we bring our blood from
Slowly dwindled; cooled
To sewage estuary, to trout-stocked tarn.
Even the Amazon's taxed and patrolled

To set laws by the few jaws –
Piranha and jaguar.
Columbus' huckstering breath
Blew inland through North America

Killing the last of the mammoths.
The right maps have no monsters.
Now the mind's wandering elementals,
Ousted from their traveller-told

Unapproachable islands,
From their heavens and their burning underworld,
Wait dully at the traffic crossing,
Or lean over headlines, taking nothing in.

Esther's Tomcat

Daylong this tomcat lies stretched flat
As an old rough mat, no mouth and no eyes,
Continual wars and wives are what
Have tattered his ears and battered his head.

Like a bundle of old rope and iron
Sleeps till blue dusk. Then reappear

His eyes, green as ringstones: he yawns wide red,
Fangs fine as a lady's needle and bright.

A tomcat sprang at a mounted knight,
Locked round his neck like a trap of hooks
While the knight rode fighting its clawing and bite.
After hundreds of years the stain's there

On the stone where he fell, dead of the tom:
That was at Barnborough. The tomcat still
Grallochs odd dogs on the quiet,
Will take the head clean off your simple pullet,

Is unkillable. From the dog's fury,
From gunshot fired point-blank he brings
His skin whole, and whole
From owlish moons of bekittenings

Among ashcans. He leaps and lightly
Walks upon sleep, his mind on the moon.
Nightly over the round world of men,
Over the roofs go his eyes and outcry.

Wilfred Owen's Photographs

When Parnell's Irish in the House
Pressed that the British Navy's cat-
O-nine-tails be abolished, what
Shut against them? It was
Neither Irish nor English nor of that
Decade, but of the species.

Predictably, Parliament
Squared against the motion. As soon
Let the old school tie be rent
Off their necks, and give thanks, as see gone
No shame but a monument –
Trafalgar not better known.

'To discontinue it were as much
As ship not powder and cannonballs
But brandy and women' (Laughter). Hearing which
A witty profound Irishman calls
For a 'cat' into the House, and sits to watch
The gentry fingering its stained tails.

Whereupon . . .
               quietly, unopposed,
The motion was passed.

Relic

I found this jawbone at the sea's edge:
There, crabs, dogfish, broken by the breakers or tossed
To flap for half an hour and turn to a crust
Continue the beginning. The deeps are cold:
In that darkness camaraderie does not hold:
Nothing touches but, clutching, devours. And the jaws,
Before they are satisfied or their stretched purpose
Slacken, go down jaws; go gnawn bare. Jaws
Eat and are finished and the jawbone comes to the beach:
This is the sea's achievement; with shells,
Vertebrae, claws, carapaces, skulls.

Time in the sea eats its tail, thrives, casts these
Indigestibles, the spars of purposes
That failed far from the surface. None grow rich
In the sea. This curved jawbone did not laugh
But gripped, gripped and is now a cenotaph.

Hawk Roosting

I sit in the top of the wood, my eyes closed.
Inaction, no falsifying dream

Between my hooked head and hooked feet:
Or in sleep rehearse perfect kills and eat.

The convenience of the high trees!
The air's buoyancy and the sun's ray
Are of advantage to me;
And the earth's face upward for my inspection.

My feet are locked upon the rough bark.
It took the whole of Creation
To produce my foot, my each feather:
Now I hold Creation in my foot

Or fly up, and revolve it all slowly –
I kill where I please because it is all mine.
There is no sophistry in my body:
My manners are tearing off heads --

The allotment of death.
For the one path of my flight is direct
Through the bones of the living.
No arguments assert my right:

The sun is behind me.
Nothing has changed since I began.
My eye has permitted no change.
I am going to keep things like this.

Fire-Eater

Those stars are the fleshed forebears
Of these dark hills, bowed like labourers,

And of my blood.

The death of a gnat is a star's mouth: its skin,
Like Mary's or Semele's, thin

As the skin of fire:
A star fell on her, a sun devoured her.

My appetite is good
Now to manage both Orion and Dog

With a mouthful of earth, my staple.
Worm-sort, root-sort, going where it is profitable.

A star pierces the slug,

The tree is caught up in the constellations.
My skull burrows among antennae and fronds.

To Paint a Water Lily

A green level of lily leaves
Roofs the pond's chamber and paves

The flies' furious arena: study
These, the two minds of this lady.

First observe the air's dragonfly
That eats meat, that bullets by

Or stands in space to take aim;
Others as dangerous comb the hum

Under the trees. There are battle-shouts
And death-cries everywhere hereabouts

But inaudible, so the eyes praise
To see the colours of these flies

Rainbow their arcs, spark, or settle
Cooling like beads of molten metal

Through the spectrum. Think what worse
Is the pond-bed's matter of course;

Prehistoric bedragonned times
Crawl that darkness with Latin names,

Have evolved no improvements there,
Jaws for heads, the set stare,

Ignorant of age as of hour –
Now paint the long-necked lily-flower

Which, deep in both worlds, can be still
As a painting, trembling hardly at all

Though the dragonfly alight,
Whatever horror nudge her root.

The Bull Moses

A hoist up and I could lean over
The upper edge of the high half-door,
My left foot ledged on the hinge, and look in at the
    byre's
Blaze of darkness: a sudden shut-eyed look
Backward into the head.
                            Blackness is depth
Beyond star. But the warm weight of his breathing,
The ammoniac reek of his litter, the hotly-tongued
Mash of his cud, steamed against me.
Then, slowly, as onto the mind's eye –
The brow like masonry, the deep-keeled neck:
Something come up there onto the brink of the gulf,
Hadn't heard of the world, too deep in itself to be called
    to,
Stood in sleep. He would swing his muzzle at a fly
But the square of sky where I hung, shouting, waving,
Was nothing to him; nothing of our light
Found any reflection in him.
                            Each dusk the farmer led him

Down to the pond to drink and smell the air,
And he took no pace but the farmer
Led him to take it, as if he knew nothing
Of the ages and continents of his fathers,
Shut, while he wombed, to a dark shed
And steps between his door and the duckpond;
The weight of the sun and the moon and the world
    hammered
To a ring of brass through his nostrils. He would raise
His streaming muzzle and look out over the meadows,
But the grasses whispered nothing awake, the fetch
Of the distance drew nothing to momentum
In the locked black of his powers. He came strolling
    gently back,
Paused neither toward the pig-pens on his right,
Nor toward the cow-byres on his left: something
Deliberate in his leisure, some beheld future
Founding in his quiet.
                    I kept the door wide,
Closed it after him and pushed the bolt.

Cat and Mouse

On the sheep-cropped summit, under hot sun,
The mouse crouched, staring out the chance
It dared not take,
                Time and a world
Too old to alter, the five mile prospect –
Woods, villages, farms – hummed its heat-heavy
Stupor of life.
                Whether to two
Feet or four, how are prayers contracted!
Whether in God's eye or the eye of a cat.

View of a Pig

The pig lay on a barrow dead.
It weighed, they said, as much as three men.
Its eyes closed, pink white eyelashes.
Its trotters stuck straight out.

Such weight and thick pink bulk
Set in death seemed not just dead.
It was less than lifeless, further off.
It was like a sack of wheat.

I thumped it without feeling remorse.
One feels guilty insulting the dead,
Walking on graves. But this pig
Did not seem able to accuse.

It was too dead. Just so much
A poundage of lard and pork.
Its last dignity had entirely gone.
It was not a figure of fun.

Too dead now to pity.
To remember its life, din, stronghold
Of earthly pleasure as it had been,
Seemed a false effort, and off the point.

Too deadly factual. Its weight
Oppressed me – how could it be moved?
And the trouble of cutting it up!
The gash in its throat was shocking, but not pathetic.

Once I ran at a fair in the noise
To catch a greased piglet
That was faster and nimbler than a cat,
Its squeal was the rending of metal.

Pigs must have hot blood, they feel like ovens.
Their bite is worse than a horse's –

They chop a half-moon clean out.
They eat cinders, dead cats.

Distinctions and admirations such
As this one was long finished with.
I stared at it a long time. They were going to scald it,
Scald it and scour it like a doorstep.

The Retired Colonel

Who lived at the top end of our street
Was a Mafeking stereotype, ageing.
Came, face pulped scarlet with kept rage,
For air past our gate.
Barked at his dog knout and whipcrack
And cowerings of India: five or six wars
Stiffened in his reddened neck;
Brow bull-down for the stroke.

Wife dead, daughters gone, lived on
Honouring his own caricature.
Shot through the heart with whisky wore
The lurch like ancient courage, would not go down
While posterity's trash stood, held
His habits like a last stand, even
As if he had Victoria rolled
In a Union Jack in that stronghold.

And what if his sort should vanish?
The rabble starlings roar upon
Trafalgar. The man-eating British lion
By a pimply age brought down.
Here's his head mounted, though only in rhymes.
Beside the head of the last English
Wolf (those starved gloomy times!)
And the last sturgeon of Thames.

November

The month of the drowned dog. After long rain the land
Was sodden as the bed of an ancient lake,
Treed with iron and birdless. In the sunk lane
The ditch – a seep silent all summer –

Made brown foam with a big voice: that, and my boots
On the lane's scrubbed stones, in the gulleyed leaves,
Against the hill's hanging silence;
Mist silvering the droplets on the bare thorns

Slower than the change of daylight.
In a let of the ditch a tramp was bundled asleep;
Face tucked down into beard, drawn in
Under his hair like a hedgehog's. I took him for dead,

But his stillness separated from the death
Of the rotting grass and the ground. A wind chilled,
And a fresh comfort tightened through him,
Each hand stuffed deeper into the other sleeve.

His ankles, bound with sacking and hairy band,
Rubbed each other, resettling. The wind hardened;
A puff shook a glittering from the thorns,
And again the rains' dragging grey columns

Smudged the farms. In a moment
The fields were jumping and smoking; the thorns
Quivered, riddled with the glassy verticals.
I stayed on under the welding cold

Watching the tramp's face glisten and the drops on his
    coat
Flash and darken. I thought what strong trust
Slept in him – as the trickling furrows slept,
And the thorn-roots in their grip on darkness;

And the buried stones, taking the weight of winter;
The hill where the hare crouched with clenched teeth.
Rain plastered the land till it was shining
Like hammered lead, and I ran, and in the rushing wood

Shuttered by a black oak leaned.
The keeper's gibbet had owls and hawks
By the neck, weasels, a gang of cats, crows:
Some, stiff, weightless, twirled like dry bark bits

In the drilling rain. Some still had their shape,
Had their pride with it; hung, chins on chests,
Patient to outwait these worst days that beat
Their crowns bare and dripped from their feet.

An Otter

I

    Underwater eyes, an eel's
Oil of water body, neither fish nor beast is the otter:
    Four-legged yet water-gifted, to outfish fish;
      With webbed feet and long ruddering tail
      And a round head like an old tomcat.

    Brings the legend of himself
From before wars or burials, in spite of hounds and
                    vermin-poles;
    Does not take root like the badger. Wanders, cries;
      Gallops along land he no longer belongs to;
      Re-enters the water by melting.

    Of neither water nor land. Seeking
Some world lost when first he dived, that he cannot
                    come at since,
    Takes his changed body into the holes of lakes;
      As if blind, cleaves the stream's push till he licks
      The pebbles of the source; from sea

To sea crosses in three nights
Like a king in hiding. Crying to the old shape of the
                                     starlit land,
   Over sunken farms where the bats go round,
   Without answer. Till light and birdsong come
   Walloping up roads with the milk wagon.

II

The hunt's lost him. Pads on mud,
Among sedges, nostrils a surface bead,
The otter remains, hours. The air,
Circling the globe, tainted and necessary,

Mingling tobacco-smoke, hounds and parsley,
Comes carefully to the sunk lungs.
So the self under the eye lies,
Attendant and withdrawn. The otter belongs

In double robbery and concealment –
From water that nourishes and drowns, and from land
That gave him his length and the mouth of the hound.
He keeps fat in the limpid integument

Reflections live on. The heart beats thick,
Big trout muscle out of the dead cold;
Blood is the belly of logic; he will lick
The fishbone bare. And can take stolen hold

On a bitch otter in a field full
Of nervous horses, but linger nowhere.
Yanked above hounds, reverts to nothing at all,
To this long pelt over the back of a chair.

Witches

Once was every woman the witch
To ride a weed the ragwort road:
Devil to do whatever she would:
Each rosebud, every old bitch.

Did they bargain their bodies or no?
Proprietary the devil that
Went horsing on their every thought
When they scowled the strong and lucky low.

Dancing in Ireland nightly, gone
To Norway (the ploughboy bridled),
Nightlong under the blackamoor spraddled,
Back beside their spouse by dawn

As if they had dreamed all. Did they dream it?
Oh, our science says they did.
It was all wishfully dreamed in bed.
Small psychology would unseam it.

Bitches still sulk, rosebuds blow,
And we are devilled. And though these weep
Over our harms, who's to know
Where their feet dance' while their heads sleep?

Thrushes

Terrifying are the attent sleek thrushes on the lawn,
More coiled steel than living – a poised
Dark deadly eye, those delicate legs
Triggered to stirrings beyond sense – with a start, a
    bounce, a stab
Overtake the instant and drag out some writhing thing.
No indolent procrastinations and no yawning stares.

No sighs or head-scratchings. Nothing but bounce and
    stab
And a ravening second.

Is it their single-mind-sized skulls, or a trained
Body, or genius, or a nestful of brats
Gives their days this bullet and automatic
Purpose? Mozart's brain had it, and the shark's mouth
That hungers down the blood-smell even to a leak of its
    own
Side and devouring of itself: efficiency which
Strikes too streamlined for any doubt to pluck at it
Or obstruction deflect.

With a man it is otherwise. Heroisms on horseback,
Outstripping his desk-diary at a broad desk,
Carving at a tiny ivory ornament
For years: his act worships itself – while for him,
Though he bends to be blent in the prayer, how loud and
    above what
Furious spaces of fire do the distracting devils
Orgy and hosannah, under what wilderness
Of black silent waters weep.

Snowdrop

Now is the globe shrunk tight
Round the mouse's dulled wintering heart.
Weasel and crow, as if moulded in brass,
Move through an outer darkness
Not in their right minds,
With the other deaths. She, too, pursues her ends,
Brutal as the stars of this month,
Her pale head heavy as metal.

Pike

Pike, three inches long, perfect
Pike in all parts, green tigering the gold.
Killers from the egg: the malevolent aged grin.
They dance on the surface among the flies.

Or move, stunned by their own grandeur
Over a bed of emerald, silhouette
Of submarine delicacy and horror.
A hundred feet long in their world.

In ponds, under the heat-struck lily pads –
Gloom of their stillness:
Logged on last year's black leaves, watching upwards.
Or hung in an amber cavern of weeds

The jaws' hooked clamp and fangs
Not to be changed at this date;
A life subdued to its instrument;
The gills kneading quietly, and the pectorals.

Three we kept behind glass,
Jungled in weed: three inches, four,
And four and a half: fed fry to them –
Suddenly there were two. Finally one.

With a sag belly and the grin it was born with.
And indeed they spare nobody.
Two, six pounds each, over two feet long,
High and dry and dead in the willow-herb –

One jammed past its gills down the other's gullet:
The outside eye stared: as a vice locks –
The same iron in this eye
Though its film shrank in death.

A pond I fished, fifty yards across,
Whose lilies and muscular tench

Had outlasted every visible stone
Of the monastery that planted them –

Stilled legendary depth:
It was as deep as England. It held
Pike too immense to stir, so immense and old
That past nightfall I dared not cast

But silently cast and fished
With the hair frozen on my head
For what might move, for what eye might move.
The still splashes on the dark pond,

Owls hushing the floating woods
Frail on my ear against the dream
Darkness beneath night's darkness had freed,
That rose slowly towards me, watching.

Sunstroke

Frightening the blood in its tunnel
The mowing machine ate at the field of grass.

My eyes had been glared dark. Through a red heat
The cradled guns, damascus, blued, flared –

At every stir sliding their molten embers
Into my head. Sleekly the clover

Bowed and flowed backward
Over the saw-set swimming blades

Till the blades bit – roots, stones, ripped into red –
Some baby's body smoking among the stalks.

Reek of paraffin oil and creosote
Swabbing my lungs doctored me back

Laid on a sack in the great-beamed engine-shed.
I drank at stone, at iron of plough and harrow;

Dulled in a pit, heard thick walls of rain
And voices in swaddled confinement near me

Warm as veins. I lay healing
Under the ragged length of a dog fox

The dangled head downward from one of the beams,
With eyes open, forepaws strained at a leap –

Also surprised by the rain.

Cleopatra to the Asp

The bright mirror I braved: the devil in it
Loved me like my soul, my soul:
Now that I seek myself in a serpent
My smile is fatal.

Nile moves in me; my thighs splay
Into the squalled Mediterranean;
My brain hides in that Abyssinia
Lost armies foundered towards.

Desert and river unwrinkle again.
Seeming to bring them the waters that make drunk
Caesar, Pompey, Antony I drank.
Now let the snake reign.

A half-deity out of Capricorn,
This rigid Augustus mounts
With his sword virginal indeed; and has shorn
Summarily the moon-horned river

From my bed. May the moon
Ruin him with virginity! Drink me, now, whole
With coiled Egypt's past; then from my delta
Swim like a fish toward Rome.

Recklings

Stealing Trout on a May Morning

I park the car half in the ditch and switch off and sit.
The hot astonishment of my engine's arrival
Sinks through 5 a.m. silence and frost.
At the end of a long gash
An atrocity through the lace of first light
I sit with the reeking instrument.
I am on delicate business.
I want the steel to be cold instantly
And myself secreted three fields away
And the farms, back under their blankets, supposing a
    plane passed.

Because this is no wilderness you can just rip into.
Every leaf is plump and well-married,
Every grain of soil of known lineage, well-connected.
And the gardens are like brides fallen asleep
Before their weddings have properly begun.
The orchards are the hushed maids, fresh from
    convent . . .
It is too hushed, something improper is going to happen.
It is too ghostly proper, all sorts of liveried listenings
Tiptoe along the lanes and peer over hedges.

I listen for the eyes jerked open on pillows,
Their dreams washed with sudden ugly petroleum.
They need only look out at a sheep.
Every sheep within two miles
Is nailing me accurately down
With its hellishly-shaven starved-priest expression.

I emerge. The air, after all, has forgotten everything.
The sugared spindles and wings of grass
Are etched on great goblets. A pigeon falls into space.
The earth is coming quietly and darkly up from a great
    depth,
Still under the surface. I am unknown,
But nothing is surprised. The tarmac of the road
Is velvet with sleep, the hills are out cold.
A new earth still in its wrappers
Of gauze and cellophane,
The frost from the storage still on its edges,
My privilege to poke and sniff.
The sheep are not much more than the primroses.
And the river there, amazed with itself,
Flexing and trying its lights
And unused fish, that are rising
And sinking for the sheer novelty
As the sun melts the hill's spine and the spilled light
Flows through their gills . . .

My mind sinks, rising and sinking.
And the opening arms of the sky forget me
Into the buried tunnel of hazels. There
My boot dangles down, till a thing black and sudden
Savages it, and the river is heaping under,
Alive and malevolent,
A coiling glider of shock, the space-black
Draining off the night-moor, under the hazels . . .
But I drop and stand square in it, against it,
Then it is river again, washing its soul,
Its stones, its weeds, its fish, its gravels
And the rooty mouths of the hazels clear
Of the discolourings bled in
Off ploughlands and lanes . . .

At first, I can hardly look at it –
The riding tables, the corrugated

Shanty roofs tightening
To braids, boilings where boulders throw up
Gestures of explosion, black splitting everywhere
To drowning skirts of whiteness, a slither of mirrors
Under the wading hazels. Here it is shallow,
Ropes my knees, lobbing fake boomerangs,
A drowned woman loving each ankle,
But I'm heavier and I wade with them upstream,
Flashing my blue minnow
Up the open throats of water
And across through the side of the rush
Of alligator escaping along there
Under the beards of the hazels, and I slice
The wild nape-hair off the bald bulges,
Till the tightrope of my first footholds
Tangles away downstream
And my bootsoles move as to magnets.

Soon I deepen. And now I meet the piling mob
Of voices and hurriers coming towards me
And tumbling past me. I press through a panic . . .
This headlong river is a rout
Of tumbrils and gun-carriages, rags and metal,
All the funeral woe-drag of some overnight disaster
Mixed with planets, electrical storms and darkness
On a mapless moorland of granite,
Trailing past me with all its frights, its eyes
With what they have seen and still see,
They drag the flag off my head, a dark insistence
Tearing the spirits from my mind's edge and from
    under . . .

To yank me clear takes the sudden, strong spine
Of one of the river's real members –
Thoroughly made of dew, lightning and granite
Very slowly over four years. A trout, a foot long,
Lifting its head in a shawl of water,

Fins banked stiff like a trireme
It forces the final curve wide, getting
A long look at me. So much for the horror
It has changed places.
                      Now I am a man in a painting
(Under the mangy, stuffed head of a fox)
Painted about 1905
Where the river steams and the frost relaxes
On the pear-blossoms. The brassy wood-pigeons
Bubble their colourful voices, and the sun
Rises upon a world well-tried and old.

Water

On moors where people get lost and die of air
On heights where the goat's stomach fails

In gorges where the toad lives on starlight
In deserts where the bone comes through the camel's
        nostril

On seas where the white bear gives up and dies of water
In depths where only the shark's tooth resists

At altitudes where the eagle would explode
Through falls of air where men become bombs

At the poles where zero is the sole hearth
Water is not lost, is snug, is at home –

Sometimes with its wife, stone –
An open-armed host, of poor cheer.

Memory

The morass is bulging and aborting –
Mother, mother, mother, what am I?

Hands of light, hands of light
Wash the writhing darkness.

Mother, the eel in the well is eating the moon!

If I stop my heart and hold my breath

The needle will thread itself.
Daring the no-man quiet of my no-being

A mouse buds at the washboarding. A nose
Of ginger spider weaves its hairs toward me.

Claws trickle onto my palm.
An ounce pins itself there,

Nose wavering to investigate me.
Am I a mouse's remembrance?

I start, and it bounces past its shadow
Into my mother's shoe

Which twists out.
                    I fly up flustered
Into the winter of a near elm.

Tutorial

Like a propped skull,
His humour is mediaeval.

What are all those tomes? Tomb-boards
Pressing the drying remains of men.
He brings some out, we stew them up to a dark amber
    and sit sipping.

He is fat, this burst bearskin, but his mind is an electric
    mantis
Plucking the heads and legs off words, the homunculi.
I am thin but I can hardly move my bulk, I go round and
    round numbly under the ice of the North Pole.

This scholar dribbling tea
Onto his tie, straining pipe-gargle
Through the wharf-weed that ennobles

The mask of enquiry, advancing into the depths like a
    harbour,
Like a sphinx cliff,
Like the papery skull of a fish

Lodged in dune sand, with a few straws,
Rifled by dry cold.
His words

Twitch and rustle, twitch
And rustle.
The scarred world looks through their gaps.

I listen
With bleak eyeholes.

Trees

I whispered to the holly . . .
There was a rustle of answer – dark,
Dark, dark, a gleamer recoiling tensely backward
Into a closing nest of shattered weapons,
Like a squid into clouds of protection.
I plucked a spiny leaf. Nothing protested.
Glints twitched, watched me.

I whispered to the birch . . .
My breath crept up into a world of shudderings.
Was she veiled?
Herself her own fountain
She pretended to be absent from it, or to be becoming air
Filtering herself from her fingertips,
Till her bole paled, like a reflection on water,
And I felt the touch of my own ghostliness –

I moved on, looking neither way,
Trying to hear
The outcry that must go with all

Those upflung maidenly gestures, that arrested humpback rout
   humpback rout
Stumbling in blackberries and bracken –

Silence.

Trees, it is your own strangeness, in the dank wood,
Makes me so horrifying
I dare not hear my own footfall.

The Lake

Better disguised than the leaf-insect,

A sort of subtler armadillo,
The lake turns with me as I walk.

Snuffles at my feet for what I might drop or kick up,
Sucks and slobbers the stones, snorts through its lips

Into broken glass, smacks its chops.
It has eaten several my size

Without developing a preference –
Prompt, with a splash, to whatever I offer.

It ruffles in its wallow, or lies sunning,
Digesting old senseless bicycles

And a few shoes. The fish down there
Do not know they have been swallowed

Any more than the girl out there, who over the stern of a rowboat
   rowboat
Tests its depth with her reflection.

Yet how the outlet fears it!

                              – dragging it out,
Black and yellow, a maniac eel,

Battering it to death with sticks and stones.

A Match

Spluttering near out, before it touches the moors,
You start, threatened by your own tears.
But not your skin, not doors, not borders
Will be proof against your foraging
Through everything unhuman or human
To savour and own the dimensions of woman
As water does those of water.
                              But the river
Is a prayer to its own waters
Where the circulation of our world is pouring
In stillness –
Everyone's peace, no less your own peace.
No movement but rooted willows.

Out of bedrock your blood's operation
Carves your eyes clear not so quickly
As your mouth dips deeper
Into the massed darkness.

Small Events

The old man's blood had spoken the word: 'Enough.'
Now nobody had the heart to see him go on.
His photographs were a cold mercy, there on the mantel.
So his mouth became a buttonhole and his limbs became
    wrapped iron.

Towards dying his eyes looked just above the things he
    looked at.
They were the poor rearguard on the beach
And turned, watering, with all his hope, from the smoke
To the sea for the Saviour

Who is useful only in life.

So, under a tree a tree-creeper, on dead grass sleeping –
It was blind, its eyes matt as blood-lice

Feeding on a raw face of disease.
I set it on dry grass, and its head fell forward, it died

Into what must have cupped it kindly.

And a grey, aged mouse, humped shivering
On the bare path, under November drizzle –
A frail parcel, delivered in damaging mail and still
      unclaimed,
Its contents no longer of use to anybody.

I picked it up. It was looking neither outward nor
      inward.
The tremendous music of its atoms
Trembled it on my fingers. As I watched it, it died.
A grey, mangy mouse, and seamed with ancient scars,

Whose blood had said: 'Sleep.'

So this year a swift's embryo, cracked too early from its
      fallen egg –
There, among mineral fragments,
The blind blood stirred,
Freed,

And, mystified, sank into hopeful sleep.

Crow Wakes

I had exploded, a bombcloud, lob-headed, my huge
      fingers
Came feeling over the fields, like shadows.
I became smaller than water, I stained into the soil-
      crumble.
I became smaller.
My eyes fell out of my head and into an atom.
My right leg stood in the room raving at me like a dog.
I tried to stifle its bloody mouth with a towel

But it ran on ahead. I stumbled after it
A long way and came to a contraption like a trap
Baited with human intestines.
A stone drummed and an eye watched me out of a cat's
    anus.
I swam upstream, cleansed, in the snow-water,
    upstream.
Till I grew tired and turned over. I slept.
When I woke I could hear voices, many voices.
It was my bones all chattering together
At the high-tide mark, bedded in rubble, littered among
    shells
And gull feathers.
                    And the breastbone was crying:
'I begat a million and murdered a million:
I was a leopard.' And 'No, no, no, no,
We were a fine woman,' a rib cried.
'No, we were swine, we had devils, and the axe halved
    us,'
The pelvis was shouting. And the bones of the feet
And the bones of the hands fought: 'We were alligators,
We dragged some beauties under, we did not let go.'
And, 'We were suffering oxen,' and 'I was a surgeon,'
And 'We were a stinking clot of ectoplasm that
    suffocated a nun
Then lay for years in a cobbler's cellar.'
The teeth sang and the vertebrae were screeching
Something incomprehensible.
                    I tried to creep away –
I got up and ran. I tried to get up and run
But they saw me. 'It's him, it's him again. Get him.'
They came howling after me and I ran.
A freezing hand caught hold of me by the hair
And lifted me off my feet and set me high
Over the whole earth on a blazing star
Called

Thistles

Against the rubber tongues of cows and the hoeing
    hands of men
Thistles spike the summer air
Or crackle open under a blue-black pressure.

Every one a revengeful burst
Of resurrection, a grasped fistful
Of splintered weapons and Icelandic frost thrust up

From the underground stain of a decayed Viking.
They are like pale hair and the gutturals of dialects.
Every one manages a plume of blood.

Then they grow grey, like men.
Mown down, it is a feud. Their sons appear,
Stiff with weapons, fighting back over the same ground.

Still Life

Outcrop stone is miserly

With the wind. Hoarding its nothings,
Letting wind run through its fingers,
It pretends to be dead of lack.
Even its grimace is empty,
Warted with quartz pebbles from the sea's womb.

It thinks it pays no rent,
Expansive in the sun's summerly reckoning.
Under rain, it gleams exultation blackly
As if receiving interest.
Similarly, it bears the snow well.

Wakeful and missing little and landmarking
The fly-like dance of the planets,
The landscape moving in sleep,
It expects to be in at the finish.
Being ignorant of this other, this harebell,

That trembles, as under threats of death,
In the summer turf's heat-rise,
And in which – filling veins
Any known name of blue would bruise
Out of existence – sleeps, recovering,

The maker of the sea.

Her Husband

Comes home dull with coal-dust deliberately
To grime the sink and foul towels and let her
Learn with scrubbing brush and scrubbing board
The stubborn character of money.

And let her learn through what kind of dust
He has earned his thirst and the right to quench it
And what sweat he has exchanged for his money
And the blood-weight of money. He'll humble her

With new light on her obligations.
The fried, woody chips, kept warm two hours in the
    oven,
Are only part of her answer.
Hearing the rest, he slams them to the fire back

And is away round the house-end singing
'Come back to Sorrento' in a voice
Of resounding corrugated iron.
Her back has bunched into a hump as an insult.

For they will have their rights.
Their jurors are to be assembled
From the little crumbs of soot. Their brief
Goes straight up to heaven and nothing more is heard of it.

Cadenza

The violinist's shadow vanishes.

The husk of a grasshopper
Sucks a remote cyclone and rises.

The full, bared throat of a woman walking water,
The loaded estuary of the dead.

And I am the cargo
Of a coffin attended by swallows.

And I am the water
Bearing the coffin that will not be silent.

The clouds are full of surgery and collision
But the coffin escapes – a black diamond,

A ruby brimming blood,
An emerald beating its shores,

The sea lifts swallow wings and flings
A summer lake open,

Sips and bewilders its reflection,
Till the whole sky dives shut like a burned land back to
    its spark –

A bat with a ghost in its mouth
Struck at by lightnings of silence –

Blue with sweat, the violinist
Crashes into the orchestra, which explodes.

Ghost Crabs

At nightfall, as the sea darkens,
A depth darkness thickens, mustering from the gulfs and
   the submarine badlands,
To the sea's edge. To begin with
It looks like rocks uncovering, mangling their pallor.
Gradually the labouring of the tide
Falls back from its productions,
Its power slips back from glistening nacelles, and they
   are crabs.
Giant crabs, under flat skulls, staring inland
Like a packed trench of helmets.
Ghosts, they are ghost-crabs.
They emerge
An invisible disgorging of the sea's cold
Over the man who strolls along the sands.
They spill inland, into the smoking purple
Of our woods and towns – a bristling surge
Of tall and staggering spectres
Gliding like shocks through water.
Our walls, our bodies, are no problem to them.
Their hungers are homing elsewhere.
We cannot see them or turn our minds from them.
Their bubbling mouths, their eyes
In a slow mineral fury
Press through our nothingness where we sprawl on
   beds,
Or sit in rooms. Our dreams are ruffled maybe,
Or we jerk awake to the world of possessions
With a gasp, in a sweat burst, brains jamming blind
Into the bulb-light. Sometimes, for minutes, a sliding
Staring
Thickness of silence
Presses between us. These crabs own this world.
All night, around us or through us,

They stalk each other, they fasten on to each other,
They mount each other, they tear each other to pieces,
They utterly exhaust each other.
They are the powers of this world.
We are their bacteria,
Dying their lives and living their deaths.
At dawn, they sidle back under the sea's edge.
They are the turmoil of history, the convulsion
In the roots of blood, in the cycles of concurrence.
To them, our cluttered countries are empty battleground.
All day they recuperate under the sea.
Their singing is like a thin sea-wind flexing in the rocks
   of a headland,
Where only crabs listen.

They are God's only toys.

Public Bar TV

On a flaked ridge of the desert

Outriders have found foul water. They say nothing;
With the cactus and the petrified tree
Crouch numbed by a wind howling all
Visible horizons equally empty.

The wind brings dust and nothing
Of the wives, the children, the grandmothers
With the ancestral bones, who months ago
Left the last river,

Coming at the pace of oxen.

Kafka

And he is an owl
He is an owl, 'Man' tattooed in his armpit
Under the broken wing
(Stunned by the wall of glare, he fell here)
Under the broken wing of huge shadow that twitches
    across the floor.
He is a man in hopeless feathers.

Second Glance at a Jaguar

Skinful of bowls he bowls them,
The hip going in and out of joint, dropping the spine
With the urgency of his hurry
Like a cat going along under thrown stones, under cover,
Glancing sideways, running
Under his spine. A terrible, stump-legged waddle
Like a thick Aztec disemboweller,
Club-swinging, trying to grind some square
Socket between his hind legs round,
Carrying his head like a brazier of spilling embers,
And the black bit of his mouth, he takes it
Between his back teeth, he has to wear his skin out,
He swipes a lap at the water-trough as he turns,
Swivelling the ball of his heel on the polished spot,
Showing his belly like a butterfly.
At every stride he has to turn a corner
In himself and correct it. His head
Is like the worn down stump of another whole jaguar,
His body is just the engine shoving it forward,
Lifting the air up and shoving on under,
The weight of his fangs hanging the mouth open,
Bottom jaw combing the ground. A gorged look,
Gangster, club-tail lumped along behind gracelessly,

He's wearing himself to heavy ovals,
Muttering some mantra, some drum-song of murder
To keep his rage brightening, making his skin
Intolerable, spurred by the rosettes, the Cain-brands,
Wearing the spots off from the inside,
Rounding some revenge. Going like a prayer-wheel,
The head dragging forward, the body keeping up,
The hind legs lagging. He coils, he flourishes
The blackjack tail as if looking for a target,
Hurrying through the underworld, soundless.

Fern

Here is the fern's frond, unfurling a gesture,
Like a conductor whose music will now be pause
And the one note of silence
To which the whole earth dances gravely.

The mouse's ear unfurls its trust,
The spider takes up her bequest,
And the retina
Reins the creation with a bridle of water.

And, among them, the fern
Dances gravely, like the plume
Of a warrior returning, under the low hills,

Into his own kingdom.

Stations

I

Suddenly his poor body
Had its drowsy mind no longer
For insulation.

Before the funeral service foundered
The lifeboat coffin had shaken to pieces
And the great stars were swimming through where he
    had been.

For a while

The stalk of the tulip at the door that had outlived him,
And his jacket, and his wife, and his last pillow
Clung to each other.

II

I can understand the haggard eyes
Of the old

Dry wrecks

Broken by seas of which they could drink nothing.

III

They have sunk into deeper service. They have gone
    down
To labour with God on the beaches. They fatten
Under the haddock's thumb. They rejoice
Through the warped mouth of the flounder

And are nowhere they are not here I know nothing
Cries the poulterer's hare hanging
Upside down above the pavement
Staring into a bloody bag. Not here

Cry the eyes from the depths

Of the mirror's seamless sand.

IV

You are a wild look – out of an egg
Laid by your absence.

In the great Emptiness you sit complacent,
Blackbird in wet snow.

If you could make only one comparison –
Your condition is miserable, you would give up.

But you, from the start, surrender to total Emptiness,
Then leave everything to it.

Absence. It is your own
Absence

Weeps its respite through your accomplished music,
Wraps its cloak dark about your feeding.

v

Whether you say it, think it, know it
Or not, it happens, it happens as
Over rails over
The neck the wheels leave
The head with its vocabulary useless,
Among the flogged plantains.

The Green Wolf

My neighbour moves less and less, attempts less.
If his right hand still moves, it is a farewell
Already days posthumous.

But the left hand seems to freeze,
And the left leg with its crude plumbing,
And the left half jaw and the left eyelid and the words all
    the huge cries

Frozen in his brain his tongue cannot unfreeze –
While somewhere through a dark heaven
The dark bloodclot moves in.

I watch it approaching but I cannot fear it.
The punctual evening star,
Worse, the warm hawthorn blossoms, their foam,

Their palls of deathly perfume,
Worst of all the beanflower
Badged with jet like the ear of the tiger

Unmake and remake me. That star
And that flower and that flower
And living mouth and living mouth all

One smouldering annihilation
Of old brains, old bowels, old bodies
In the scarves of dew, the wet hair of nightfall.

The Bear

In the huge, wide-open, sleeping eye of the mountain
The bear is the gleam in the pupil
Ready to awake
And instantly focus.

The bear is glueing
Beginning to end
With glue from people's bones
In his sleep.

The bear is digging
In his sleep
Through the wall of the Universe
With a man's femur.

The bear is a well
Too deep to glitter
Where your shout
Is being digested.

The bear is a river
Where people bending to drink
See their dead selves.

The bear sleeps
In a kingdom of walls
In a web of rivers.

He is the ferryman
To dead land.

His price is everything.

Scapegoats and Rabies

I A HAUNTING

Soldiers are marching singing down the lane

They get their abandon
From the fixed eyes of girls, from their own
Armed anonymity
And from having finally paid up
All life might demand. They get
Their heroic loom
From the statue stare of old women,
From the trembling chins of old men,
From the napes and bow legs of toddlers,
From the absolute steel
Of their automatic rifles, and the lizard spread
Of their own fingers, and from their bird stride.
They get their facelessness
From the blank, deep meadows and the muddling
   streams
And the hill's eyeless outlook,
The babel of gravestones, the mouldering
Of letters and citations

On rubbish dumps. They get the drumming engine
Of their boots
From their hearts,
From their eyeless, earless hearts,
Their brainless hearts. And their bravery
From the dead millions of ghosts
Marching in their boots, cumbering their bodies,
Staring from under their brows, concentrating
Toward a repeat performance. And their hopelessness
From the millions of the future
Marching in their boots, blindfold and riddled,
Rotten heads on their singing shoulders,
The blown-off right hand swinging to the stride
Of the stump-scorched and blown-off legs
Helpless in the terrible engine of the boots.

The soldiers go singing down the deep lane
Wraiths into the bombardment of afternoon sunlight,
Whelmed under the flashing onslaught of the barley,
Strangled in the drift of honeysuckle.

Their bodiless voices rally on the slope and again
In the far woods

Then settle like dust
Under the ancient burden of the hill.

II THE MASCOT

Somewhere behind the lines, over the map,
The General's face hangs in the dark, like a lantern.

Every shell that bursts
Blows it momentarily out, and he has to light it.

Every bullet that bangs off
Goes in at one of his ears and out at the other.

Every attack every rout
Storms through that face, like a flood through a
   footbridge.

Every new-dead ghost
Comes to that worn-out blood for its death-ration.

Every remotest curse, weighted with a bloodclot,
Enters that ear like a blowfly.

Knives, forks, spoons divide his brains.
The supporting earth, and the night around him,

Smoulder like the slow, curing fire
Of a Javanese head-shrinker.

Nothing remains of the *tête d'armée* but the skin –
A dangling parchment lantern

Slowly revolving to right, revolving to left,

Trembling a little with the incessant pounding,

Over the map, empty in the ring of light.

III WIT'S END

The General commits his emptiness to God.

And in place of his eyes
Crystal balls
Roll with visions.

And his voice rises
From the dead fragments of men

A Frankenstein
A tank
A ghost
Roaming the impossible
Raising the hair on men's heads.

His hand
Has swept the battlefield flat as a sheet of foolscap.
He writes:

I AM A LANTERN
              IN THE HAND
                          OF A BLIND PEOPLE

IV TWO MINUTES' SILENCE

The soldier's boots, beautifully bulled,
Are graves
On the assembly line
Rolls Royces
Opera boxes
Double beds
Safes
With big smiles and laced-up eyes

His stockings
Are his own intestines
Cut into lengths –
They wear better and are
Nobody else's loss,
So he needn't charge diffidently

His battledress
Is Swanwhite's undies
Punch and Judy curtains
The Queen's pajamas
The Conjuror's hankie

The flapping sheet
Of the shithouse phantom

His helmet
Is a Ministry pisspot

His rifle
Is a Thames turd

And away downwind he runs, over no man's land,
In a shouting flight
From his own stink

Into the mushroom forest

Watched from the crowded walls.

V THE RED CARPET

So the leaves trembled.

He leaned for a moment
Into the head-on leaden blast of ghost
From death's doorway
Then fell forward, under his equipment.
But though the jungle morass has gripped him to the
    knees
His outflung left hand clawed and got a hold
On Notting Hill
His brow banged hard down once then settled gently
Onto Hampstead Heath
The thumb of his twisted, smashed right hand
Settled in numb snugness
Across the great doorway of St Paul's
His lips oozed soft words and blood bubbles
Into the Chalk Farm railway cutting
Westminster knuckled his riddled chest
His belt-buckle broke Clapham
His knees his knees were dissolving in the ebb of the
    Channel
And there he lay alive
His body full of lights, the restaurants seethed,
He groaned in the pushing of traffic that would not end
The girls strolled and their perfumes gargled in his throat

And in the holes in his chest
And though he could not lift his eyes to the streetlights
And though he could not stir either hand
He knew in that last stride, that last
Ten thousand league effort, and even off balance,
He had made it home. And he called –

Into mud.

Again the leaves trembled.

Splinters flew off Big Ben.

Theology

No, the serpent did not
Seduce Eve to the apple.
All that's simply
Corruption of the facts.

Adam ate the apple.
Eve ate Adam.
The serpent ate Eve.
This is the dark intestine.

The serpent, meanwhile,
Sleeps his meal off in Paradise –
Smiling to hear
God's querulous calling.

Gog

I woke to a shout: 'I am Alpha and Omega.'
Rocks and a few trees trembled
Deep in their own country.
I ran and an absence bounded beside me.

The dog's god is a scrap dropped from the table.
The mouse's saviour is a ripe wheat grain.
Hearing the Messiah cry
My mouth widens in adoration.

How fat are the lichens!
They cushion themselves on the silence.
The air wants for nothing.
The dust, too, is replete.

What was my error? My skull has sealed it out.
My great bones are massed in me.
They pound on the earth, my song excites them.
I do not look at the rocks and trees, I am frightened of
     what they see.

I listen to the song jarring my mouth
Where the skull-rooted teeth are in possession.
I am massive on earth. My feetbones beat on the earth
Over the sounds of motherly weeping . . .

Afterwards I drink at a pool quietly.
The horizon bears the rocks and trees away into twilight.
I lie down. I become darkness.

Darkness that all night sings and circles stamping.

Kreutzer Sonata

Now you have stabbed her good
A flower of unknown colour appallingly
Blackened by your surplus of bile
Blooms wetly on her dress.

'Your mystery! Your mystery! . . .'
All facts, with all absence of facts,
Exhale as the wound there
Drinks its roots and breathes them to nothing.

71

Vile copulation! Vile! – etcetera.
But now your dagger has outdone everybody's.
Say goodbye, for your wife's sweet flesh goes off,
Booty of the envious spirit's assault.

A sacrifice, not a murder.
One hundred and forty pounds
Of excellent devil, for God.
She tormented Ah demented you

With that fat lizard Trukachevsky,
That fiddling, leering penis.
Yet why should you castrate yourself
To be rid of them both?

Now you have stabbed her good
Trukachevsky is cut off
From any further operation on you.
And she can find nobody else.

Rest in peace, Tolstoy!
It must have taken supernatural greed
To need to corner all the meat in the world,
Even from your own hunger.

Out

My father sat in his chair recovering
From the four-year mastication by gunfire and mud,
Body buffeted wordless, estranged by long soaking
In the colours of mutilation.
                                   His outer perforations
Were valiantly healed, but he and the hearth-fire, its
    blood-flicker
On biscuit-bowl and piano and table leg,

Moved into strong and stronger possession
Of minute after minute, as the clock's tiny cog
Laboured and on the thread of his listening
Dragged him bodily from under
The mortised four-year strata of dead Englishmen
He belonged with. He felt his limbs clearing
With every slight, gingerish movement. While I, small
    and four,
Lay on the carpet as his luckless double,
His memory's buried, immovable anchor,
Among jawbones and blown-off boots, tree-stumps,
    shellcases and craters,
Under rain that goes on drumming its rods and
    thickening
Its kingdom, which the sun has abandoned, and where
    nobody
Can ever again move from shelter.

II

The dead man in his cave beginning to sweat;
The melting bronze visor of flesh
Of the mother in the baby-furnace –
Nobody believes, it
Could be nothing, all
Undergo smiling at
The lulling of blood in
Their ears, their ears, their ears, their eyes
Are only drops of water and even the dead man
    suddenly
Sits up and sneezes – Atishoo!
Then the nurse wraps him up, smiling,
And, though faintly, the mother is smiling,
And it's just another baby.

As after being blasted to bits
The reassembled infantryman

Tentatively totters out, gazing around with the eyes
Of an exhausted clerk.

III REMEMBRANCE DAY

The poppy is a wound, the poppy is the mouth
Of the grave, maybe of the womb searching –

A canvas-beauty puppet on a wire
Today whoring everywhere. It is years since I wore one.

It is more years
The shrapnel that shattered my father's paybook

Gripped me, and all his dead
Gripped him to a time

He no more than they could outgrow, but, cast into one,
    like iron,
Hung deeper than refreshing of ploughs

In the woe-dark under my mother's eye –
One anchor

Holding my juvenile neck bowed to the dunkings of the
    Atlantic.

So goodbye to that bloody-minded flower.

You dead bury your dead.
Goodbye to the cenotaphs on my mother's breasts.

Goodbye to all the remaindered charms of my father's
    survival.

Let England close. Let the green sea-anemone close.

New Moon in January

A splinter, flicked
Into the wide eyeball,
Severs its warning.

The head, severed while staring,
Felt nothing, only
Tilted slightly.

O lone
Eyelash on the darkening
Stripe of blood, O sail of death!

Frozen
In ether
Unearthly

Shelley's faint-shriek
Trying to thaw while zero
Itself loses consciousness.

The Warriors of the North

Bringing their frozen swords, their salt-bleached eyes,
    their salt-bleached hair,
The snow's stupefied anvils in rows,
Bringing their envy,
The slow ships feelered Southward, snails over the steep
    sheen of the water-globe.

Thawed at the red and black disgorging of abbeys,
The bountiful, cleft casks,
The fluttered bowels of the women of dead burghers,
And the elaborate, patient gold of the Gaels.

To no end
But this timely expenditure of themselves,

A cash-down, beforehand revenge, with extra,
For the gruelling relapse and prolongueur of their blood

Into the iron arteries of Calvin.

Song of a Rat

I THE RAT'S DANCE

The rat is in the trap, it is in the trap,
And attacking heaven and earth with a mouthful of
   screeches like torn tin,

An effective gag.
When it stops screeching, it pants

And cannot think
'This has no face, it must be God' or

'No answer is also an answer.'
Iron jaws, strong as the whole earth

Are stealing its backbone
For a crumpling of the Universe with screechings,

For supplanting every human brain inside its skull with a
   rat-body that knots and unknots,
A rat that goes on screeching,

Trying to uproot itself into each escaping screech,
But its long fangs bar that exit –

The incisors bared to the night spaces, threatening the
   constellations,
The glitterers in the black, to keep off,

Keep their distance,
While it works this out.

The rat understands suddenly. It bows and is still,
With a little beseeching of blood on its nose-end.

II THE RAT'S VISION

The rat hears the wind saying something in the straw
And the night-fields that have come up to the fence,
    leaning their silence,
The widowed land
With its trees that know how to cry

The rat sees the farm bulk of beam and stone
Wobbling like reflection on water.
The wind is pushing from the gulf
Through the old barbed wire, in through the trenched
    gateway, past the gates of the ear, deep into the
    worked design of days,

Breathes onto the solitary snow crystal

The rat screeches
And 'Do not go' cry the dandelions, from their heads of
    folly
And 'Do not go' cry the yard cinders, who have no
    future, only their infernal aftermath
And 'Do not go' cries the cracked trough by the gate,
    fatalist of starlight and zero

'Stay' says the arrangement of stars

Forcing the rat's head down into godhead.

III THE RAT'S FLIGHT

The heaven shudders, a flame unrolled like a whip,
And the stars jolt in their sockets.
And the sleep-souls of eggs
Wince under the shot of shadow –

That was the Shadow of the Rat
Crossing into power
Never to be buried

The horned Shadow of the Rat
Casting here by the door
A bloody gift for the dogs

While it supplants Hell.

Heptonstall

Black village of gravestones.
Skull of an idiot
Whose dreams die back
Where they were born.

Skull of a sheep
Whose meat melts
Under its own rafters.
Only the flies leave it.

Skull of a bird,
The great geographies
Drained to sutures
Of cracked windowsills.

Life tries.

Death tries.

The stone tries.

Only the rain never tires.

Skylarks

I

The lark begins to go up
Like a warning
As if the globe were uneasy –

Barrel-chested for heights,
Like an Indian of the high Andes,

A whippet head, barbed like a hunting arrow,

But leaden
With muscle
For the struggle
Against
Earth's centre.

And leaden
For ballast
In the rocketing storms of the breath.

Leaden
Like a bullet
To supplant
Life from its centre.

II

Crueller than owl or eagle

A towered bird, shot through the crested head
With the command, Not die

But climb

Climb

Sing

Obedient as to death a dead thing.

III

I suppose you just gape and let your gaspings
Rip in and out through your voicebox
                              O lark

And sing inwards as well as outwards
Like a breaker of ocean milling the shingle
                                    O lark

O song, incomprehensibly both ways –
Joy! Help! Joy! Help!
                    O lark

IV

You stop to rest, far up, you teeter
Over the drop

But not stopping singing

Resting only for a second

Dropping just a little

Then up and up and up

Like a mouse with drowning fur
Bobbing and bobbing at the well-wall

Lamenting, mounting a little –

But the sun will not take notice
And the earth's centre smiles.

V

My idleness curdles
Seeing the lark labour near its cloud
Scrambling
In a nightmare difficulty
Up through the nothing

Its feathers thrash, its heart must be drumming like a
    motor,
As if it were too late, too late

Dithering in ether
Its song whirls faster and faster
And the sun whirls
The lark is evaporating
Till my eye's gossamer snaps
         and my hearing floats back widely to earth

After which the sky lies blank open
Without wings, and the earth is a folded clod.

Only the sun goes silently and endlessly on with the
    lark's song.

VI

All the dreary Sunday morning
Heaven is a madhouse
With the voices and frenzies of the larks,

Squealing and gibbering and cursing

Heads flung back, as I see them,
Wings almost torn off backwards – far up

Like sacrifices set floating
The cruel earth's offerings

The mad earth's missionaries.

VII

Like those flailing flames
That lift from the fling of a bonfire
Claws dangling full of what they feed on

The larks carry their tongues to the last atom
Battering and battering their last sparks out at the limit –
So it's a relief, a cool breeze
When they've had enough, when they're burned out

And the sun's sucked them empty
And the earth gives them the O.K.

And they relax, drifting with changed notes

Dip and float, not quite sure if they may
Then they are sure and they stoop

And maybe the whole agony was for this

The plummeting dead drop

With long cutting screams buckling like razors

But just before they plunge into the earth

They flare and glide off low over grass, then up
To land on a wall-top, crest up,

Weightless,
Paid-up,
Alert,

Conscience perfect.

VIII

Manacled with blood,
Cuchulain listened bowed,
Strapped to his pillar (not to die prone)
Hearing the far crow
Guiding the near lark nearer
With its blind song

'That some sorry little wight more feeble and misguided than
    thyself
Take thy head
Thine ear
And thy life's career from thee.'

Pibroch

The sea cries with its meaningless voice
Treating alike its dead and its living,
Probably bored with the appearance of heaven
After so many millions of nights without sleep,
Without purpose, without self-deception.

Stone likewise. A pebble is imprisoned
Like nothing in the Universe.
Created for black sleep. Or growing
Conscious of the sun's red spot occasionally,
Then dreaming it is the foetus of God.

Over the stone rushes the wind
Able to mingle with nothing,
Like the hearing of the blind stone itself.
Or turns, as if the stone's mind came feeling
A fantasy of directions.

Drinking the sea and eating the rock
A tree struggles to make leaves –
An old woman fallen from space
Unprepared for these conditions.
She hangs on, because her mind's gone completely.

Minute after minute, aeon after aeon,
Nothing lets up or develops.
And this is neither a bad variant nor a tryout.
This is where the staring angels go through.
This is where all the stars bow down.

The Howling of Wolves

Is without world.

What are they dragging up and out on their long leashes
  of sound
That dissolve in the mid-air silence?

Then crying of a baby, in this forest of starving silences,
Brings the wolves running.
Tuning of a viola, in this forest delicate as an owl's ear,
Brings the wolves running – brings the steel traps
  clashing and slavering,
The steel furred to keep it from cracking in the cold,
The eyes that never learn how it has come about
That they must live like this,

That they must live

Innocence crept into minerals.

The wind sweeps through and the hunched wolf shivers.
It howls you cannot say whether out of agony or joy.

The earth is under its tongue,
A dead weight of darkness, trying to see through its
  eyes.
The wolf is living for the earth.
But the wolf is small, it comprehends little.

It goes to and fro, trailing its haunches and whimpering
  horribly.

It must feed its fur.

The night snows stars and the earth creaks.

Gnat-Psalm

When the gnats dance at evening
Scribbling on the air, sparring sparely,
Scrambling their crazy lexicon,
Shuffling their dumb Cabala,
Under leaf shadow

Leaves only leaves
Between them and the broad swipes of the sun
Leaves muffling the dusty stabs of the late sun
From their frail eyes and crepuscular temperaments

Dancing
Dancing
Writing on the air, rubbing out everything they write
Jerking their letters into knots, into tangles
Everybody everybody else's yoyo

Immense magnets fighting around a centre

Not writing and not fighting but singing
That the cycles of this Universe are no matter
That they are not afraid of the sun
That the one sun is too near
It blasts their song, which is of all the suns
That they are their own sun
Their own brimming over
At large in the nothing
Their wings blurring the blaze
Singing

That they are the nails
In the dancing hands and feet of the gnat-god
That they hear the wind suffering
Through the grass
And the evening tree suffering

The wind bowing with long cat-gut cries
And the long roads of dust
Dancing in the wind
The wind's dance, the death-dance, entering the
    mountain
And the cow dung villages huddling to dust

But not the gnats, their agility
Has outleaped that threshold
And hangs them a little above the claws of the grass
Dancing
Dancing
In the glove shadows of the sycamore

A dance never to be altered
A dance giving their bodies to be burned

And their mummy faces will never be used

Their little bearded faces
Weaving and bobbing on the nothing
Shaken in the air, shaken, shaken
And their feet dangling like the feet of victims

O little Hasids
Ridden to death by your own bodies
Riding your bodies to death
You are the angels of the only heaven!

And God is an Almighty Gnat!
You are the greatest of all the galaxies!
My hands fly in the air, they are follies
My tongue hangs up in the leaves
My thoughts have crept into crannies

Your dancing

Your dancing

Rolls my staring skull slowly away into outer space.

Full Moon and Little Frieda

A cool small evening shrunk to a dog bark and the clank
of a bucket –

And you listening.
A spider's web, tense for the dew's touch.
A pail lifted, still and brimming – mirror
To tempt a first star to a tremor.

Cows are going home in the lane there, looping the
hedges with their warm wreaths of breath –
A dark river of blood, many boulders,
Balancing unspilled milk.

'Moon!' you cry suddenly, 'Moon! Moon!'

The moon has stepped back like an artist gazing amazed
at a work

That points at him amazed.

Wodwo

What am I? Nosing here, turning leaves over
Following a faint stain on the air to the river's edge
I enter water. What am I to split
The glassy grain of water looking upward I see the bed
Of the river above me upside down very clear
What am I doing here in mid-air? Why do I find
this frog so interesting as I inspect its most secret
interior and make it my own? Do these weeds
know me and name me to each other have they
seen me before, do I fit in their world? I seem
separate from the ground and not rooted but dropped
out of nothing casually I've no threads
fastening me to anything I can go anywhere

I seem to have been given the freedom
of this place what am I then? And picking
bits of bark off this rotten stump gives me
no pleasure and it's no use so why do I do it
me and doing that have coincided very queerly
But what shall I be called am I the first
have I an owner what shape am I what
shape am I am I huge if I go
to the end on this way past these trees and past these
    trees
till I get tired that's touching one wall of me
for the moment if I sit still how everything
stops to watch me I suppose I am the exact centre
but there's all this what is it roots
roots roots roots and here's the water
again very queer but I'll go on looking

from CROW

Two Legends

I

Black was the without eye
Black the within tongue
Black was the heart
Black the liver, black the lungs
Unable to suck in light
Black the blood in its loud tunnel
Black the bowels packed in furnace
Black too the muscles
Striving to pull out into the light
Black the nerves, black the brain
With its tombed visions
Black also the soul, the huge stammer
Of the cry that, swelling, could not
Pronounce its sun.

II

Black is the wet otter's head, lifted.
Black is the rock, plunging in foam.
Black is the gall lying on the bed of the blood.

Black is the earth-globe, one inch under,
An egg of blackness
Where sun and moon alternate their weathers

To hatch a crow, a black rainbow
Bent in emptiness
                    over emptiness

But flying

Lineage

In the beginning was Scream
Who begat Blood
Who begat Eye
Who begat Fear
Who begat Wing
Who begat Bone
Who begat Granite
Who begat Violet
Who begat Guitar
Who begat Sweat
Who begat Adam
Who begat Mary
Who begat God
Who begat Nothing
Who begat Never
Never Never Never

Who begat Crow

Screaming for Blood
Grubs, crusts
Anything

Trembling featherless elbows in the nest's filth

Examination at the Womb-Door

Who owns these scrawny little feet?   *Death.*
Who owns this bristly scorched-looking face?   *Death.*
Who owns these still-working lungs?   *Death.*
Who owns this utility coat of muscles?   *Death.*
Who owns these unspeakable guts?   *Death.*
Who owns these questionable brains?   *Death.*
All this messy blood?   *Death.*

These minimum-efficiency eyes?   *Death.*
This wicked little tongue?   *Death.*
This occasional wakefulness?   *Death.*

Given, stolen, or held pending trial?
Held.

Who owns the whole rainy, stony earth?   *Death.*
Who owns all of space?   *Death.*

Who is stronger than hope?   *Death.*
Who is stronger than the will?   *Death.*
Stronger than love?   *Death.*
Stronger than life?   *Death.*

But who is stronger than death?
                                        Me, evidently.

Pass, Crow.

A Childish Prank

Man's and woman's bodies lay without souls,
Dully gaping, foolishly staring, inert
On the flowers of Eden.
God pondered.

The problem was so great, it dragged him asleep.

Crow laughed.
He bit the Worm, God's only son,
Into two writhing halves.

He stuffed into man the tail half
With the wounded end hanging out.

He stuffed the head half headfirst into woman
And it crept in deeper and up
To peer out through her eyes

Calling its tail-half to join up quickly, quickly
Because O it was painful.

Man awoke being dragged across the grass.
Woman awoke to see him coming.
Neither knew what had happened.

God went on sleeping.

Crow went on laughing.

Crow's First Lesson

God tried to teach Crow how to talk.
'Love,' said God. 'Say, Love.'
Crow gaped, and the white shark crashed into the sea
And went rolling downwards, discovering its own
    depth.

'No, no,' said God. 'Say Love. Now try it. LOVE.'
Crow gaped, and a bluefly, a tsetse, a mosquito
Zoomed out and down
To their sundry flesh-pots.

'A final try,' said God. 'Now, LOVE.'
Crow convulsed, gaped, retched and
Man's bodiless prodigious head
Bulbed out onto the earth, with swivelling eyes,
Jabbering protest –

And Crow retched again, before God could stop him.
And woman's vulva dropped over man's neck and
    tightened.
The two struggled together on the grass.
God struggled to part them, cursed, wept –

Crow flew guiltily off.

That Moment

When the pistol muzzle oozing blue vapour
Was lifted away
Like a cigarette lifted from an ashtray

And the only face left in the world
Lay broken
Between hands that relaxed, being too late

And the trees closed forever
And the streets closed forever

And the body lay on the gravel
Of the abandoned world
Among abandoned utilities
Exposed to infinity forever

Crow had to start searching for something to eat.

Crow Tyrannosaurus

Creation quaked voices –
It was a cortege
Of mourning and lament
Crow could hear and he looked around fearfully.

The swift's body fled past
Pulsating
With insects
And their anguish, all it had eaten.

The cat's body writhed
Gagging
A tunnel
Of incoming death-struggles, sorrow on sorrow.

And the dog was a bulging filterbag
Of all the deaths it had gulped for the flesh and the
    bones.
It could not digest their screeching finales.
Its shapeless cry was a blort of all those voices.

Even man he was a walking
Abattoir
Of innocents –
His brain incinerating their outcry.

Crow thought 'Alas
Alas ought I
To stop eating
And try to become the light?'

But his eye saw a grub. And his head, trapsprung,
    stabbed.
And he listened
And he heard
Weeping

Grubs grubs He stabbed   he stabbed
Weeping
Weeping

Weeping he walked and stabbed

Thus came the eye's
                    roundness
                            the ear's
                                    deafness.

The Black Beast

Where is the Black Beast?
Crow, like an owl, swivelled his head.
Where is the Black Beast?

Crow hid in its bed, to ambush it.
Where is the Black Beast?
Crow sat in its chair, telling loud lies against the Black
    Beast.
Where is it?
Crow shouted after midnight, pounding the wall with a
    last.
Where is the Black Beast?
Crow split his enemy's skull to the pineal gland.
Where is the Black Beast?

Crow crucified a frog under a microscope, he peered into
    the brain of a dogfish.
Where is the Black Beast?

Crow roasted the earth to a clinker, he charged into
    space –
Where is the Black Beast?

The silences of space decamped, space flitted in every
    direction –
Where is the Black Beast?

Crow flailed immensely through the vacuum, he
    screeched after the disappearing stars –
Where is it? Where is the Black Beast?

Crow's Account of the Battle

There was this terrific battle.
The noise was as much
As the limits of possible noise could take.
There were screams higher groans deeper
Than any ear could hold.
Many eardrums burst and some walls
Collapsed to escape the noise.
Everything struggled on its way

Through this tearing deafness
As through a torrent in a dark cave.

The cartridges were banging off, as planned,
The fingers were keeping things going
According to excitement and orders.
The unhurt eyes were full of deadliness.
The bullets pursued their courses
Through clods of stone, earth and skin,
Through intestines, pocket-books, brains, hair, teeth
According to Universal laws.
And mouths cried 'Mamma'
From sudden traps of calculus,
Theorems wrenched men in two,
Shock-severed eyes watched blood
Squandering as from a drain-pipe
Into the blanks between stars.
Faces slammed down into clay
As for the making of a life-mask
Knew that even on the sun's surface
They could not be learning more or more to the point.
Reality was giving its lesson,
Its mishmash of scripture and physics,
With here, brains in hands, for example,
And there, legs in a treetop.

There was no escape except into death.
And still it went on – it outlasted
Many prayers, many a proved watch,
Many bodies in excellent trim,
Till the explosives ran out
And sheer weariness supervened
And what was left looked round at what was left.

Then everybody wept,
Or sat, too exhausted to weep,
Or lay, too hurt to weep.

And when the smoke cleared it became clear
This had happened too often before
And was going to happen too often in future
And happened too easily
Bones were too like lath and twigs
Blood was too like water
Cries were too like silence
The most terrible grimaces too like footprints in mud
And shooting somebody through the midriff
Was too like striking a match
Too like potting a snooker ball
Too like tearing up a bill
Blasting the whole world to bits
Was too like slamming a door
Too like dropping in a chair
Exhausted with rage
Too like being blown to bits yourself
Which happened too easily
With too like no consequences.

So the survivors stayed.
And the earth and the sky stayed.
Everything took the blame.

Not a leaf flinched, nobody smiled.

Crow's Fall

When Crow was white he decided the sun was too
      white.
He decided it glared much too whitely.
He decided to attack it and defeat it.

He got his strength flush and in full glitter.
He clawed and fluffed his rage up.
He aimed his beak direct at the sun's centre.

97

He laughed himself to the centre of himself

And attacked.

At his battle cry trees grew suddenly old,
Shadows flattened.

But the sun brightened –
It brightened, and Crow returned charred black.

He opened his mouth but what came out was charred
black.

'Up there,' he managed,
'Where white is black and black is white, I won.'

Crow and the Birds

When the eagle soared clear through a dawn distilling of
emerald.
When the curlew trawled in seadusk through a chime of
wineglasses
When the swallow swooped through a woman's song in
a cavern
And the swift flicked through the breath of a violet

When the owl sailed clear of tomorrow's conscience
And the sparrow preened himself of yesterday's promise
And the heron laboured clear of the Bessemer upglare
And the bluetit zipped clear of lace panties
And the woodpecker drummed clear of the rotovator and
the rose-farm
And the peewit tumbled clear of the laundromat

While the bullfinch plumped in the apple bud
And the goldfinch bulbed in the sun
And the wryneck crooked in the moon
And the dipper peered from the dewball

Crow spraddled head-down in the beach-garbage,
guzzling a dropped ice-cream.

Crow on the Beach

Hearing shingle explode, seeing it skip,
Crow sucked his tongue.
Seeing sea-grey mash a mountain of itself
Crow tightened his goose-pimples.
Feeling spray from the sea's root nothinged on his crest
Crow's toes gripped the wet pebbles.
When the smell of the whale's den, the gulfing of the
    crab's last prayer,
Gimletted in his nostril
He grasped he was on earth.
                              He knew he grasped
Something fleeting
Of the sea's ogreish outcry and convulsion.
He knew he was the wrong listener unwanted
To understand or help --

His utmost gaping of brain in his tiny skull
Was just enough to wonder, about the sea,

What could be hurting so much?

The Contender

There was this man and he was the strongest
Of the strong.
He gritted his teeth like a cliff.
Though his body was sweeling away like a torrent on a
    cliff
Smoking towards dark gorges
There he nailed himself with nails of nothing

All the women in the world could not move him
They came their mouths deformed against stone
They came and their tears salted his nail-holes
Only adding their embitterment
To his effort
He abandoned his grin to them his grimace
In his face upwards body he lay face downwards
As a dead man adamant

His sandals could not move him they burst their thongs
And rotted from his fixture
All the men in the world could not move him
They wore at him with their shadows and little sounds
Their arguments were a relief
Like heather flowers
His belt could not endure the siege – it burst
And lay broken
He grinned
Little children came in chorus to move him
But he glanced at them out of his eye-corners
Over the edge of his grin
And they lost their courage for life

Oak forests came and went with the hawk's wing
Mountains rose and fell
He lay crucified with all his strength
On the earth
Grinning towards the sun
Through the tiny holes of his eyes
And towards the moon
And towards the whole paraphernalia of the heavens
Through the seams of his face
With the strings of his lips
Grinning through his atoms and decay
Grinning into the black

Into the ringing nothing
Through the bones of his teeth

Sometimes with eyes closed

In his senseless trial of strength.

Crow's Vanity

Looking close in the evil mirror Crow saw
Mistings of civilizations   towers   gardens
Battles he wiped the glass   but there came

Mistings of skyscrapers   webs of cities
Steaming the glass he wiped it   there came

Spread of swampferns fronded on the mistings
A trickling spider   he wiped the glass   he peered

For a glimpse of the usual grinning face

But it was no good he was breathing too heavy
And too hot   and space was too cold

And here came the misty ballerinas
The burning gulfs   the hanging gardens   it was eerie

A Horrible Religious Error

When the serpent emerged, earth-bowel brown,
From the hatched atom
With its alibi self twisted around it

Lifting a long neck
And balancing that deaf and mineral stare
The sphinx of the final fact

And flexing on that double flameflicker tongue
A syllable like the rustling of the spheres

God's grimace writhed, a leaf in the furnace

And man's and woman's knees melted, they collapsed
Their neck-muscles melted, their brows bumped the
    ground
Their tears evacuated visibly
They whispered 'Your will is our peace.'

But Crow only peered.
                    Then took a step or two forward,
Grabbed this creature by the slackskin nape,

Beat the hell out of it, and ate it.

In Laughter

Cars collide and erupt luggage and babies
In laughter
The steamer upends and goes under saluting like a
    stuntman
In laughter
The nosediving aircraft concludes with a boom
In laughter
People's arms and legs fly off and fly on again
In laughter
The haggard mask on the bed rediscovers its pang
In laughter, in laughter
The meteorite crashes
With extraordinarily ill-luck on the pram

The ears and eyes are bundled up
Are folded up in the hair,
Wrapped in the carpet, the wallpaper, tied with the
    lampflex

Only the teeth work on
And the heart, dancing on in its open cave
Helpless on the strings of laughter

While the tears are nickel-plated and come through doors
   with a bang

And the wails stun with fear
And the bones
Jump from the torment flesh has to stay for

Stagger some distance and fall in full view

Still laughter scampers around on centipede boots
Still it runs all over on caterpillar tread
And rolls back onto the mattress, legs in the air

But it's only human

And finally it's had enough – enough!
And slowly sits up, exhausted,
And slowly starts to fasten buttons,
With long pauses,

Like somebody the police have come for.

Robin Song

I am the hunted king
  Of the frost and big icicles
    And the bogey cold
    With its wind boots.

I am the uncrowned
  Of the rainworld
    Hunted by lightning and thunder
    And rivers.

I am the lost child
  Of the wind
    Who goes through me looking for something else
    Who can't recognize me though I cry.

I am the maker
  Of the world
    That rolls to crush
    And silence my knowledge.

Conjuring in Heaven

So finally there was nothing.
It was put inside nothing.
Nothing was added to it
And to prove it didn't exist
Squashed flat as nothing with nothing.

Chopped up with a nothing
Shaken in a nothing
Turned completely inside out
And scattered over nothing –
So everybody saw that it was nothing
And that nothing more could be done with it

And so it was dropped. Prolonged applause in Heaven.

It hit the ground and broke open –

There lay Crow, cataleptic.

Owl's Song

He sang
How the swan blanched forever
How the wolf threw away its telltale heart
And the stars dropped their pretence

The air gave up appearances
Water went deliberately numb
The rock surrendered its last hope
And cold died beyond knowledge

He sang
How everything had nothing more to lose

Then sat still with fear

Seeing the clawtrack of star
Hearing the wingbeat of rock

And his own singing

Crow's Elephant Totem Song

Once upon a time
God made this Elephant.
Then it was delicate and small
It was not freakish at all
Or melancholy

The Hyenas sang in the scrub: You are beautiful –
They showed their scorched heads and grinning
    expressions
Like the half-rotted stumps of amputations –
We envy your grace
Waltzing through the thorny growth
O take us with you to the Land of Peaceful
O ageless eyes of innocence and kindliness
Lift us from the furnaces
And furies of our blackened faces
Within these hells we writhe
Shut in behind the bars of our teeth
In hourly battle with a death
The size of the earth
Having the strength of the earth.

So the Hyenas ran under the Elephant's tail
As like a lithe and rubber oval
He strolled gladly around inside his ease
But he was not God no it was not his
To correct the damned
In rage in madness then they lit their mouths
They tore out his entrails
They divided him among their several hells
To cry all his separate pieces
Swallowed and inflamed
Amidst paradings of infernal laughter.

At the Resurrection
The Elephant got himself together with correction
Deadfall feet and toothproof body and bulldozing bones
And completely altered brains
Behind aged eyes, that were wicked and wise.

So through the orange blaze and blue shadow
Of the afterlife, effortless and immense,
The Elephant goes his own way, a walking sixth sense,
And opposite and parallel
The sleepless Hyenas go
Along a leafless skyline trembling like an oven roof
With a whipped run
Their shame-flags tucked hard down
Over the gutsacks
Crammed with putrefying laughter
Blotched black with the leakage and seepings
And they sing: 'Ours is the land
Of loveliness and beautiful
Is the putrid mouth of the leopard
And the graves of fever
Because it is all we have –'
And they vomit their laughter.

And the Elephant sings deep in the forest-maze
About a star of deathless and painless peace
But no astronomer can find where it is.

Dawn's Rose

Is melting an old frost moon.

Agony under agony, the quiet of dust,
And a crow talking to stony skylines.

Desolate is the crow's puckered cry
As an old woman's mouth
When the eyelids have finished
And the hills continue.

A cry
Wordless
As the newborn baby's grieving
On the steely scales.

As the dull gunshot and its after-râle
Among conifers, in rainy twilight.

Or the suddenly dropped, heavily dropped
Star of blood on the fat leaf.

The Smile

Began under the groan of the oldest forest
It ran through the clouds, a third light
And it ran through the skin of the earth

It came circling the earth
Like the lifted bow
Of a wave's submarine running
Tossing the willows, and swelling the elm-tops
Looking for its occasion

107

But people were prepared
They met it
With visor smiles, mirrors of ricochet
With smiles that stole a bone
And smiles that went off with a mouthful of blood
And smiles that left poison in a numb place
Or doubled up
Covering a getaway

But the smile was too vast, it outflanked all
It was too tiny it slipped between the atoms
So that the steel screeched open
Like a gutted rabbit, the skin was nothing
Then the pavement and the air and the light
Confined all the jumping blood
No better than a paper bag
People were running with bandages
But the world was a draughty gap
The whole creation
Was just a broken gutter pipe

And there was the unlucky person's eye
Pinned under its brow
Widening for the darkness behind it
Which kept right on getting wider, darker
As if the soul were not working

And at that very moment the smile arrived

And the crowd, shoving to get a glimpse of a man's soul
Stripped to its last shame,
Met this smile
That rose through his torn roots
Touching his lips, altering his eyes
And for a moment
Mending everything

Before it swept out and away across the earth.

Crow's Battle Fury

When the patient, shining with pain,
Suddenly pales,
Crow makes a noise suspiciously like laughter.

Seeing the night-city, on the earth's blue bulge,
Trembling its tambourine,
He bellows laughter till the tears come.

Remembering the painted masks and the looming of the
    balloons
Of the pinpricked dead
He rolls on the ground helpless.

And he sees his remote feet and he chokes he
Holds his aching sides –
He can hardly bear it.

One of his eyes sinks into his skull, tiny as a pin,
One opens, a gaping dish of pupils,
His temple-veins gnarl, each like the pulsing head of a
    month-old baby,
His heels double to the front,
His lips lift off his cheekbone, his heart and his liver fly
    in his throat,
Blood blasts from the crown of his head in a column –

Such as cannot be in this world.

A hair's breadth out of the world

He comes forward a step,
                    and a step,
                            and a step –

Crow Blacker than Ever

When God, disgusted with man,
Turned towards Heaven,
And man, disgusted with God,
Turned towards Eve,
Things looked like falling apart.

But Crow   Crow
Crow nailed them together,
Nailing Heaven and earth together –

So man cried, but with God's voice.
And God bled, but with man's blood.

Then Heaven and earth creaked at the joint
Which became gangrenous and stank –
A horror beyond redemption.

The agony did not diminish.

Man could not be man nor God God.

The agony

Grew.

Crow

Grinned

Crying: 'This is my Creation,'

Flying the black flag of himself.

Revenge Fable

There was a person
Could not get rid of his mother
As if he were her topmost twig.
So he pounded and hacked at her

With numbers and equations and laws
Which he invented and called truth.
He investigated, incriminated
And penalized her, like Tolstoy,
Forbidding, screaming and condemning,
Going for her with a knife,
Obliterating her with disgusts
Bulldozers and detergents
Requisitions and central heating
Rifles and whisky and bored sleep.

With all her babes in her arms, in ghostly weepings,
She died.

His head fell off like a leaf.

Bedtime Anecdote

There was a man
Who got up from a bed that was no bed
Who pulled on his clothes that were no clothes
(A million years whistling in his ear)
And he pulled on shoes that were no shoes
Carefully jerking the laces tight – and tighter
To walk over floors that were no floor
Down stairs that were no stairs
Past pictures that were no pictures
To pause
To remember and forget the night's dreams that were no
    dreams

And there was the cloud, primeval, the prophet;
There was the rain, its secret writing, the water-kernel
Of the tables of the sun;
And there was the light with its loose rant;
There were the birch trees, insisting and urging.

And the wind, reproach upon reproach.
At the table he cupped his eyes in his hands
As if to say grace

Avoiding his reflection in the mirror
Huddled to read news that was no news
(A million years revolving on his stomach)
He entered the circulation of his life
But stopped reading feeling the weight of his hand
In the hand that was no hand
And he did not know what to do or where to begin
To live the day that was no day

And Brighton was a picture
The British Museum was a picture
The battleship off Flamborough was a picture
And the drum-music the ice in the glass the mouths
Stretched open in laughter
That was no laughter
Were what was left of a picture

In a book
Under a monsoon downpour
In a ruinous mountain hut

From which years ago his body was lifted by a leopard.

Apple Tragedy

So on the seventh day
The serpent rested.
God came up to him.
'I've invented a new game,' he said.

The serpent stared in surprise
At this interloper.
But God said: 'You see this apple?
I squeeze it and look – Cider.'

The serpent had a good drink
And curled up into a questionmark.
Adam drank and said: 'Be my god.'
Eve drank and opened her legs

And called to the cockeyed serpent
And gave him a wild time.
God ran and told Adam
Who in drunken rage tried to hang himself in the
    orchard.

The serpent tried to explain, crying 'Stop'
But drink was splitting his syllable
And Eve started screeching: 'Rape! Rape!'
And stamping on his head.

Now whenever the snake appears she screeches
'Here it comes again! Help! O help!'
Then Adam smashes a chair on its head,
And God says: 'I am well pleased'

And everything goes to hell.

Crow's Last Stand

Burning
        burning
                burning
                        there was finally something
The sun could not burn, that it had rendered
Everything down to – a final obstacle
Against which it raged and charred

And rages and chars

Limpid among the glaring furnace clinkers
The pulsing blue tongues and the red and the yellow
The green lickings of the conflagration

Limpid and black –

Crow's eye-pupil, in the tower of its scorched fort.

Fragment of an Ancient Tablet

Above – the well-known lips, delicately downed.
Below – beard between thighs.

Above – her brow, the notable casket of gems.
Below – the belly with its blood-knot.

Above – many a painful frown.
Below – the ticking bomb of the future.

Above – her perfect teeth, with the hint of a fang at the
    corner.
Below – the millstones of two worlds.

Above – a word and a sigh.
Below – gouts of blood and babies.

Above – the face, shaped like a perfect heart.
Below – the heart's torn face.

Lovesong

He loved her and she loved him
His kisses sucked out her whole past and future or tried
    to
He had no other appetite
She bit him she gnawed him she sucked
She wanted him complete inside her

Safe and sure forever and ever
Their little cries fluttered into the curtains

Her eyes wanted nothing to get away
Her looks nailed down his hands his wrists his elbows
He gripped her hard so that life
Should not drag her from that moment
He wanted all future to cease
He wanted to topple with his arms round her
Off that moment's brink and into nothing
Or everlasting or whatever there was
Her embrace was an immense press
To print him into her bones
His smiles were the garrets of a fairy palace
Where the real world would never come
Her smiles were spider bites
So he would lie still till she felt hungry
His words were occupying armies
Her laughs were an assassin's attempts
His looks were bullets daggers of revenge
Her glances were ghosts in the corner with horrible
    secrets
His whispers were whips and jackboots
Her kisses were lawyers steadily writing
His caresses were the last hooks of a castaway
Her love-tricks were the grinding of locks
And their deep cries crawled over the floors
Like an animal dragging a great trap

His promises were the surgeon's gag
Her promises took the top off his skull
She would get a brooch made of it
His vows pulled out all her sinews
He showed her how to make a love-knot
Her vows put his eyes in formalin
At the back of her secret drawer
Their screams stuck in the wall

115

Their heads fell apart into sleep like the two halves
Of a lopped melon, but love is hard to stop

In their entwined sleep they exchanged arms and legs
In their dreams their brains took each other hostage

In the morning they wore each other's face

Notes for a Little Play

First – the sun coming closer, growing by the minute.
Next – clothes torn off.
Without a goodbye
Faces and eyes evaporate.
Brains evaporate.
Hands arms legs feet head and neck
Chest and belly vanish
With all the rubbish of the earth.

And the flame fills all space.
The demolition is total
Except for two strange items remaining in the flames –
Two survivors, moving in the flames blindly.

Mutations – at home in the nuclear glare.

Horrors – hairy and slobbery, glossy and raw.

They sniff towards each other in the emptiness.

They fasten together. They seem to be eating each other.

But they are not eating each other.

They do not know what else to do.

They have begun to dance a strange dance.

And this is the marriage of these simple creatures –
Celebrated here, in the darkness of the sun,

Without guest or God.

The Lovepet

Was it an animal was it a bird?
She stroked it. He spoke to it softly.
She made her voice its happy forest.
He brought it out with sugarlump smiles.
Soon it was licking their kisses.

She gave it the strings of her voice which it swallowed
He gave it the blood of his face it grew eager
She gave it the liquorice of her mouth it began to thrive
He opened the aniseed of his future
And it bit and gulped, grew vicious, snatched
The focus of his eyes
She gave it the steadiness of her hand
He gave it the strength of his spine it ate everything

It began to cry what could they give it
They gave it their calendars it bolted their diaries
They gave it their sleep it gobbled their dreams
Even while they slept
It ate their bodyskin and the muscle beneath
They gave it vows its teeth clashed its starvation
Through every word they uttered

It found snakes under the floor it ate them
It found a spider horror
In their palms and ate it

They gave it double smiles and blank silence
It chewed holes in their carpets
They gave it logic
It ate the colour of their hair
They gave it every argument that would come
They gave it shouting and yelling they meant it
It ate the faces of their children
They gave it their photograph albums they gave it their
    records

It ate the colour of the sun
They gave it a thousand letters they gave it money
It ate their future complete it waited for them
Staring and starving
They gave it screams it had gone too far
It ate into their brains
It ate the roof
It ate lonely stone it ate wind crying famine
It went furiously off

They wept they called it back it could have everything
It stripped out their nerves chewed chewed flavourless
It bit at their numb bodies they did not resist
It bit into their blank brains they hardly knew

It moved bellowing
Through a ruin of starlight and crockery

It drew slowly off they could not move

It went far away they could not speak

How Water Began to Play

Water wanted to live
It went to the sun it came weeping back
Water wanted to live
It went to the trees they burned it came weeping back
They rotted it came weeping back
Water wanted to live
It went to the flowers they crumpled it came weeping
    back
It wanted to live
It went to the womb it met blood
It came weeping back
It went to the womb it met knife
It came weeping back

It went to the womb it met maggot and rottenness
It came weeping back it wanted to die

It went to time it went through the stone door
It came weeping back
It went searching through all space for nothingness
It came weeping back it wanted to die

Till it had no weeping left

It lay at the bottom of all things

Utterly worn out   utterly clear

Littleblood

O littleblood, hiding from the mountains in the
    mountains
Wounded by stars and leaking shadow
Eating the medical earth.

O littleblood, little boneless little skinless
Ploughing with a linnet's carcase
Reaping the wind and threshing the stones.

O littleblood, drumming in a cow's skull
Dancing with a gnat's feet
With an elephant's nose with a crocodile's tail.

Grown so wise grown so terrible
Sucking death's mouldy tits.

Sit on my finger, sing in my ear, O littleblood.

from CAVE BIRDS

The Scream

There was the sun on the wall – my childhood's
Nursery picture. And there my gravestone
Shared my dreams, and ate and drank with me happily.

All day the hawk perfected its craftsmanship
And even through the night the miracle persisted.

Mountains lazed in their smoky camp.
Worms in the ground were doing a good job.

Flesh of bronze, stirred with a bronze thirst,
Like a newborn baby at the breast,
Slept in the sun's mercy.

And the inane weights of iron
That come suddenly crashing into people, out of
     nowhere,
Only made me feel brave and creaturely.

When I saw little rabbits with their heads crushed on
     roads
I knew I rode the wheel of the galaxy.

Calves' heads all dew-bristled with blood on counters
Grinned like masks where sun and moon danced.

And my mate with his face sewn up
Where they'd opened it to take something out
Lifted a hand –

He smiled, in half-coma,
A stone temple smile.

Then I, too, opened my mouth to praise –

But a silence wedged my gullet.

Like an obsidian dagger, dry, jag-edged,
A silent lump of volcanic glass,

The scream
Vomited itself.

The Executioner

Fills up
Sun, moon, stars, he fills them up

With his hemlock –
They darken

He fills up the evening and the morning, they darken
He fills up the sea

He comes in under the blind filled-up heaven
Across the lightless filled-up face of water

He fills up the rivers he fills up the roads, like tentacles
He fills up the streams and the paths, like veins

The tap drips darkness darkness
Sticks to the soles of your feet

He fills up the mirror, he fills up the cup
He fills up your thoughts to the brims of your eyes

You just see he is filling the eyes of your friends
And now lifting your hand you touch at your eyes

Which he has completely filled up
You touch him

You have no idea what has happened
To what is no longer yours

It feels like the world
Before your eyes ever opened

The Knight

Has conquered. He has surrendered everything.

Now he kneels. He is offering up his victory
And unlacing his steel.

In front of him are the common wild stones of the earth –

The first and last altar
Onto which he lowers his spoils.

And that is right. He has conquered in earth's name.
Committing these trophies

To the small madness of roots, to the mineral stasis
And to rain.

An unearthly cry goes up.
The Universes squabble over him –

Here a bone, there a rag.
His sacrifice is perfect. He reserves nothing.

Skylines tug him apart, winds drink him,
Earth itself unravels him from beneath –

His submission is flawless.

Blueflies lift off his beauty.
Beetles and ants officiate

Pestering him with instructions.
His patience grows only more vast.

His eyes darken bolder in their vigil
As the chapel crumbles.

His spine survives its religion,
The texts moulder –

The quaint courtly language
Of wingbones and talons.

And already
Nothing remains of the warrior but his weapons

And his gaze.
Blades, shafts, unstrung bows – and the skull's beauty

Wrapped in the rags of his banner.
He is himself his banner and its rags.

While hour by hour the sun
Deepens its revelation.

A Flayed Crow in the Hall of Judgement

All darkness comes together, rounding an egg.
Darkness in which there is now nothing.

A blot has knocked me down. It clogs me.
A globe of blot, a drop of unbeing.

Nothingness came close and breathed on me – a frost
A shawl of annihilation curls me up like a shrimpish
    foetus.

I rise beyond height – I fall past falling.
I float on a nowhere
As mist-balls float, and as stars.

A condensation, a gleam simplification
Of all that pertained.
This cry alone struggles in its tissues.

Where am I going? What will come to me here?
Is this everlasting? Is it
Stoppage and the start of nothing?

Or am I under attention?
Do purposeful cares incubate me?
Am I the self of some spore

In this white of death blackness,
This yoke of afterlife?
What feathers shall I have? What is my weakness

Good for? Great fear
Rests on the thing I am, as a feather on a hand.

I shall not fight
Against whatever is allotted to me.

My soul skinned, and my soul-skin pinned out
A mat for my judges.

The Guide

When everything that can fall has fallen
Something rises.
And leaving here, and evading there
And that, and this, is my headway.

Where the snow glare blinded you
I start.
Where the snow mama cuddled you warm
I fly up. I lift you.

Tumbling worlds
Open my way

And you cling.

And we go

Into the wind. The flame-wind – a red wind
And a black wind. The red wind comes
To empty you. And the black wind, the longest wind
The headwind

To scour you.

125

Then the non-wind, a least breath,
Fills you from easy sources.

I am the needle

Magnetic
A tremor

The searcher
The finder

His Legs Ran About

Till they seemed to trip and trap
Her legs in a single tangle

His arms lifted things, felt through dark rooms, at last
    with their hands
Caught her arms
And lay down enwoven at last at last

His chest pushed until it came against
Her breasts at the end of everything

His navel fitted over her navel as closely as possible
Like a mirror face down flat on a mirror

And so when every part
Like a bull pressing towards its cows, not to be stayed
Like a calf seeking its mama
Like a desert staggerer, among his hallucinations
Finding the hoof-churned hole

Finally got what it needed, and grew still, and closed its
    eyes

Then such truth and greatness descended

As over a new grave, when the mourners have gone
And the stars come out
And the earth, bristling and raw, tiny and lost
Resumes its search

Rushing through the vast astonishment.

Bride and Groom Lie Hidden for Three Days

She gives him his eyes, she found them
Among some rubble, among some beetles

He gives her her skin
He just seemed to pull it down out of the air and lay it
  over her
She weeps with fearfulness and astonishment

She has found his hands for him, and fitted them freshly
  at the wrists
They are amazed at themselves, they go feeling all over
  her

He has assembled her spine, he cleaned each piece
  carefully
And sets them in perfect order
A superhuman puzzle but he is inspired
She leans back twisting this way and that, using it and
  laughing, incredulous

Now she has brought his feet, she is connecting them
So that his whole body lights up

And he has fashioned her new hips
With all fittings complete and with newly wound coils,
  all shiningly oiled
He is polishing every part, he himself can hardly believe
  it

They keep taking each other to the sun, they find they
   can easily
To test each new thing at each new step

And now she smooths over him the plates of his skull
So that the joints are invisible
And now he connects her throat, her breasts and the pit
   of her stomach
With a single wire

She gives him his teeth, tying their roots to the centrepin
   of his body

He sets the little circlets on her fingertips

She stitches his body here and there with steely purple
   silk

He oils the delicate cogs of her mouth

She inlays with deep-cut scrolls the nape of his neck

He sinks into place the inside of her thighs

So, gasping with joy, with cries of wonderment
Like two gods of mud
Sprawling in the dirt, but with infinite care

They bring each other to perfection.

The Risen

He stands, filling the doorway
In the shell of earth.

He lifts wings, he leaves the remains of something,
A mess of offal, muddled as an afterbirth.

His each wingbeat – a convict's release.
What he carries will be plenty.

He slips behind the world's brow
As music escapes its skull, its clock and its skyline.

Under his sudden shadow, flames cry out among
    thickets.
When he soars, his shape

Is a cross, eaten by light,
On the Creator's face.

He shifts world weirdly as sunspots
Emerge as earthquakes.

A burning unconsumed,
A whirling tree –

Where he alights
A skin sloughs from a leafless apocalypse.

On his lens
Each atom engraves with a diamond.

In the wind-fondled crucible of his splendour
The dirt becomes God.

But when will he land
On a man's wrist.

from SEASON SONGS

A March Calf

Right from the start he is dressed in his best – his blacks
    and his whites
Little Fauntleroy – quiffed and glossy,
A Sunday suit, a wedding natty get-up,
Standing in dunged straw

Under cobwebby beams, near the mud wall,
Half of him legs,
Shining-eyed, requiring nothing more
But that mother's milk come back often.

Everything else is in order, just as it is.
Let the summer skies hold off, for the moment.
This is just as he wants it.
A little at a time, of each new thing, is best.

Too much and too sudden is too frightening –
When I block the light, a bulk from space,
To let him in to his mother for a suck,
He bolts a yard or two, then freezes,

Staring from every hair in all directions,
Ready for the worst, shut up in his hopeful religion,
A little syllogism
With a wet blue-reddish muzzle, for God's thumb.

You see all his hopes bustling
As he reaches between the worn rails towards
The topheavy oven of his mother.
He trembles to grow, stretching his curl-tip tongue –

What did cattle ever find here
To make this dear little fellow
So eager to prepare himself?
He is already in the race, and quivering to win –

His new purpled eyeball swivel-jerks
In the elbowing push of his plans.
Hungry people are getting hungrier,
Butchers developing expertise and markets,

But he just wobbles his tail – and glistens
Within his dapper profile
Unaware of how his whole lineage
Has been tied up.

He shivers for feel of the world licking his side.
He is like an ember – one glow
Of lighting himself up
With the fuel of himself, breathing and brightening.

Soon he'll plunge out, to scatter his seething joy,
To be present at the grass,
To be free on the surface of such a wideness,
To find himself himself. To stand. To moo.

The River in March

Now the river is rich, but her voice is low.
It is her Mighty Majesty the sea
Travelling among the villages incognito.

Now the river is poor. No song, just a thin mad whisper.
The winter floods have ruined her.
She squats between draggled banks, fingering her rags
    and rubbish.

And now the river is rich. A deep choir.
It is the lofty clouds, that work in heaven,
Going on their holiday to the sea.

The river is poor again. All her bones are showing.
Through a dry wig of bleached flotsam she peers up
    ashamed
From her slum of sticks.

Now the river is rich, collecting shawls and minerals.
Rain brought fatness, but she takes ninety-nine percent
Leaving the fields just one percent to survive on.

And now she is poor. Now she is East wind sick.
She huddles in holes and corners. The brassy sun gives
    her a headache.
She has lost all her fish. And she shivers.

But now once more she is rich. She is viewing her lands.
A hoard of king-cups spills from her folds, it blazes, it
    cannot be hidden.
A salmon, a sow of solid silver,

Bulges to glimpse it.

Apple Dumps

After the fiesta, the beauty-contests, the drunken
    wrestling
Of the blossom
Come some small ugly swellings, the dwarfish truths
Of the prizes.

After blushing and confetti, the breeze-blown
    bridesmaids, the shadowed snapshots
Of the trees in bloom
Come the gruelling knuckles, and the cracked
    housemaid's hands,
The workworn morning plainness of apples.

Unearthly was the hope, the wet star melting the gland,
Staggering the offer –
But pawky the real returns, not easy to see,
Dull and leaf-green, hidden, still-bitter, and hard.

The orchard flared wings, a new heaven, a dawn-lipped
   apocalypse
Kissing the sleeper –
The apples emerge, in the sun's black shade, among
   stricken trees,
A straggle of survivors, nearly all ailing.

Swifts

Fifteenth of May. Cherry blossom. The swifts
Materialize at the tip of a long scream
Of needle. 'Look! They're back! Look!' And they're gone
On a steep

Controlled scream of skid
Round the house-end and away under the cherries. Gone.
Suddenly flickering in sky summit, three or four
   together,
Gnat-whisp frail, and hover-searching, and listening

For air-chills – are they too early? With a bowing
Power-thrust to left, then to right, then a flicker they
Tilt into a slide, a tremble for balance,
Then a lashing down disappearance

Behind elms.
               They've made it again,
Which means the globe's still working, the Creation's
Still waking refreshed, our summer's
Still all to come –
                    And here they are, here they are again
Erupting across yard stones

Shrapnel-scatter terror. Frog-gapers,
Speedway goggles, international mobsters –

A bolas of three or four wire screams
Jockeying across each other
On their switchback wheel of death.
They swat past, hard-fletched,

Veer on the hard air, toss up over the roof,
And are gone again. Their mole-dark labouring,
Their lunatic limber scramming frenzy
And their whirling blades

Sparkle out into blue –
                            Not ours any more.
Rats ransacked their nests so now they shun us.
Round luckier houses now
They crowd their evening dirt-track meetings,

Racing their discords, screaming as if speed-burned,
Head-height, clipping the doorway
With their leaden velocity and their butterfly lightness,
Their too much power, their arrow-thwack into the
        eaves.

Every year a first-fling, nearly-flying
Misfit flopped in our yard,
Groggily somersaulting to get airborne.
He bat-crawled on his tiny useless feet, tangling his flails

Like a broken toy, and shrieking thinly
Till I tossed him up – then suddenly he flowed away
        under
His bowed shoulders of enormous swimming power,
Slid away along levels wobbling

On the fine wire they have reduced life to,
And crashed among the raspberries.
Then followed fiery hospital hours
In a kitchen. The moustached goblin savage

Nested in a scarf. The bright blank
Blind, like an angel, to my meat-crumbs and flies.
Then eyelids resting. Wasted clingers curled.
The inevitable balsa death.
                              Finally burial
For the husk
Of my little Apollo –

The charred scream
Folded in its huge power.

Sheep

I

The sheep has stopped crying.
All morning in her wire-mesh compound
On the lawn, she has been crying
For her vanished lamb. Yesterday they came.
Then her lamb could stand, in a fashion,
And make some tiptoe cringing steps.
Now he has disappeared.
He was only half the proper size,
And his cry was wrong. It was not
A dry little hard bleat, a baby-cry
Over a flat tongue, it was human,
It was a despairing human smooth Oh!
Like no lamb I ever heard. Its hindlegs
Cowered in under its lumped spine,
Its feeble hips leaned towards
Its shoulders for support. Its stubby
White wool pyramid head, on a tottery neck,
Had sad and defeated eyes, pinched, pathetic,
Too small, and it cried all the time
Oh! Oh! staggering towards
Its alert, baffled, stamping, storming mother

Who feared our intentions. He was too weak
To find her teats, or to nuzzle up in under,
He hadn't the gumption. He was fully
Occupied just standing, then shuffling
Towards where she'd removed to. She knew
He wasn't right, she couldn't
Make him out. Then his rough-curl legs,
So stoutly built, and hooved
With real quality tips,
Just got in the way, like a loose bundle
Of firewood he was cursed to manage,
Too heavy for him, lending sometimes
Some support, but no strength, no real help.
When we sat his mother on her tail, he mouthed her
    teat,
Slobbered a little, but after a minute
Lost aim and interest, his muzzle wandered,
He was managing a difficulty
Much more urgent and important. By evening
He could not stand. It was not
That he could not thrive, he was born
With everything but the will –
That can be deformed, just like a limb.
Death was more interesting to him.
Life could not get his attention.
So he died, with the yellow birth-mucus
Still in his cardigan.
He did not survive a warm summer night.
Now his mother has started crying again.
The wind is oceanic in the elms
And the blossom is all set.

II

What is it this time the dark barn again
Where men jerk me off my feet

And shout over me with murder voices
And do something painful to somewhere on my body

Why am I grabbed by the leg and dragged from my
    friends
Where I was hidden safe though it was hot
Why am I dragged into the light and whirled onto my
    back
Why am I sat up on my rear end with my legs splayed

A man grips me helpless his knees grip me helpless
What is that buzzer what is it coming
Buzzing like a big fierce insect on a long tangling of
    snake
What is the man doing to me with his buzzing thing

That I cannot see he is pressing it into me
I surrender I let my legs kick I let myself be killed

I let him hoist me about he twists me flat
In a leverage of arms and legs my neck pinned under his
    ankle

While he does something dreadful down the whole
    length of my belly
My little teats stand helpless and terrified as he buzzes
    around them

Poor old ewe! She peers around from her ridiculous
    position.
Cool intelligent eyes, of grey-banded agate and amber,

Eyes deep and clear with feeling and understanding
While her monster hooves dangle helpless
And a groan like no bleat vibrates in her squashed
    windpipe
And the cutter buzzes at her groin and her fleece piles
    away

Now it buzzes at her throat and she emerges whitely
More and more grotesquely female and nude
Paunchy and skinny, while her old rug, with its foul
    tassels
Heaps from her as a foam-stiff, foam-soft, yoke-yellow
    robe

Numbed all over she suddenly feels much lighter
She feels herself free, her legs are her own and she
    scrambles up
Waiting for that grapple of hands to fling her down again
She stands in the opened arch of his knees she is facing a
    bright doorway

With a real bleat to comfort the lamb in herself
She trots across the threshold and makes one high
    clearing bound
To break from the cramp of her fright
And surprised by her new lightness and delighted

She trots away, noble-nosed, her pride unsmirched.
Her greasy winter-weight stays coiled on the foul floor,
    for somebody else to bother about.
She has a beautiful wet green brand on her bobbing
    brand-new backside,
She baas, she has come off best.

III

The mothers have come back
From the shearing, and behind the hedge
The woe of sheep is like a battlefield
In the evening, when the fighting is over,
And the cold begins, and the dew falls,
And bowed women move with water.
Mother mother mother the lambs
Are crying, and the mothers are crying.
Nothing can resist that probe, that cry

Of a lamb for its mother, or an ewe's crying
For its lamb. The lambs cannot find
Their mothers among those shorn strangers.
A half-hour they have lamented,
Shaking their voices in desperation.
Bald brutal-voiced mothers braying out,
Flat-tongued lambs chopping off hopelessness.
Their hearts are in panic, their bodies
Are a mess of woe, woe they cry,
They mingle their trouble, a music
Of worse and worse distress, a worse entangling,
They hurry out little notes
With all their strength, cries searching this way and that.
The mothers force out sudden despair, blaaa!
On restless feet, with wild heads.

Their anguish goes on and on, in the June heat.
Only slowly their hurt dies, cry by cry,
As they fit themselves to what has happened.

Evening Thrush

Beyond a twilight of limes and willows
The church craftsman is still busy –
Switing idols,
Rough pre-Goidelic gods and goddesses,
Out of old bits of churchyard yew.

Suddenly flinging
Everything off, head-up, flame-naked,
Plunges shuddering into the creator –

Then comes plodding back, with a limp, over cobbles.

That was a virtuoso's joke.

Now, serious, stretched full height, he aims
At the zenith. He situates a note
Right on the source of light.

Sews a seamless garment, simultaneously
Hurls javelins of dew
Three in air together, catches them.

Explains a studied theorem of sober practicality.

Cool-eyed,
Gossips in a mundane code of splutters
With Venus and Jupiter.
                              Listens –
Motionless, intent astronomer.

Suddenly launches a soul –

The first roses hang in a yoke stupor.
Globe after globe rolls out
Through his fluteful of dew –

The tree-stacks ride out on the widening arc.

Alone and darkening
At the altar of a star
With his sword through his throat
The thrush of clay goes on arguing
Over the graves.

O thrush,
If that really is you, behind the leaf-screen,
Who is this –

Worn-headed, on the lawn's grass, after sunset,
Humped, voiceless, turdus, imprisoned
As a long-distance lorry-driver, dazed

With the pop and static and unending
Of worms and wife and kids?

The Harvest Moon

The flame-red moon, the harvest moon,
Rolls along the hills, gently bouncing,
A vast balloon,
Till it takes off, and sinks upward
To lie in the bottom of the sky, like a gold doubloon.

The harvest moon has come,
Booming softly through heaven, like a bassoon.
And earth replies all night, like a deep drum.

So people can't sleep,
So they go out where elms and oak trees keep
A kneeling vigil, in a religious hush.
The harvest moon has come!

And all the moonlit cows and all the sheep
Stare up at her petrified, while she swells
Filling heaven, as if red hot, and sailing
Closer and closer like the end of the world.

Till the gold fields of stiff wheat
Cry 'We are ripe, reap us!' and the rivers
Sweat from the melting hills.

Leaves

Who's killed the leaves?
Me, says the apple, I've killed them all.
Fat as a bomb or a cannonball
I've killed the leaves.

Who sees them drop?
Me, says the pear, they will leave me all bare
So all the people can point and stare.
I see them drop.

Who'll catch their blood?
Me, me, me, says the marrow, the marrow.
I'll get so rotund that they'll need a wheelbarrow.
I'll catch their blood.

Who'll make their shroud?
Me, says the swallow, there's just time enough
Before I must pack all my spools and be off.
I'll make their shroud.

Who'll dig their grave?
Me, says the river, with the power of the clouds
A brown deep grave I'll dig under my floods.
I'll dig their grave.

Who'll be their parson?
Me, says the Crow, for it is well known
I study the bible right down to the bone.
I'll be their parson.

Who'll be chief mourner?
Me, says the wind, I will cry through the grass
The people will pale and go cold when I pass.
I'll be chief mourner.

Who'll carry the coffin?
Me, says the sunset, the whole world will weep
To see me lower it into the deep.
I'll carry the coffin.

Who'll sing a psalm?
Me, says the tractor, with my gear-grinding glottle
I'll plough up the stubble and sing through my throttle.
I'll sing the psalm.

Who'll toll the bell?
Me, says the robin, my song in October
Will tell the still gardens the leaves are over.
I'll toll the bell.

from Autumn Notes

III

The chestnut splits its padded cell.
It opens an African eye.

A cabinet-maker, an old master
In the root of things, has done it again.

Its slippery gloss is a swoon,
A peek over the edge into – what?

Down the well-shaft of swirly grain,
Past the generous hands that lifted the May-lamps,

Into the Fairytale of a royal tree
That does not know about conkers

Or the war-games of boys.
Invisible though he is, this plump mare

Bears a tall armoured rider towards
The mirk-forest of rooty earth.

He rides to fight the North corner.
He must win a sunbeam princess

From the cloud castle of the rains.
If he fails, evil faces,

Jaws without eyes, will tear him to pieces.
If he succeeds, and has the luck

To snatch his crown from the dragon
Which resembles a slug

He will reign over our garden
For two hundred years.

IV

When the Elm was full
When it heaved and all its tautnesses drummed
Like a full-sail ship

It was just how I felt.
Waist-deep, I ploughed through the lands,
I leaned at horizons, I bore down on strange harbours.

As the sea is a sail-ship's root
So the globe was mine.
When the swell lifted the crow from the Elm-top
Both Poles were my home, they rocked me and supplied
    me.

But now the Elm is still
All its frame bare
Its leaves are a carpet for the cabbages

And it stands engulfed in the peculiar golden light
With which Eternity's flash
Photographed the sudden cock pheasant –

Engine whinneying, the fire-ball bird clatters up,
Shuddering full-throttle
Its three-tongued tail-tip writhing

And the Elm stands, astonished, wet with light,

And I stand, dazzled to my bones, blinded.

v

Through all the orchard's boughs
A honey-colour stillness, a hurrying stealth,
A quiet migration of all that can escape now.

Under ripe apples, a snapshot album is smouldering.

With a bare twig,
Glow-dazed, I coax its stubborn feathers.
A gold furred flame. A blue tremor of the air.

The fleshless faces dissolve, one by one,
As they peel open. Blackenings shrivel
To grey flutter. The clump's core hardens. Everything

Has to be gone through. Every corpuscle
And its gleam. Everything must go.
My heels squeeze wet mulch, and my crouch aches.

A wind-swell lifts through the oak.
Scorch-scathed, crisping, a fleeing bonfire
Hisses in invisible flames – and the flame-roar.

An alarmed blackbird, lean, alert, scolds
The everywhere slow exposure – flees, returns.

VI

Water-wobbling blue-sky-puddled October.
The distance microscopic, the ditches brilliant.
Flowers so low-powered and fractional
They are not in any book.

I walk on high fields feeling the bustle
Of the million earth-folk at their fair.
Fieldfares early, exciting foreigners.
A woodpigeon pressing over, important as a policeman.

A far Bang! Then Bang! and a litter of echoes –
Country pleasures. The farmer's guest,
In U.S. combat green, will be trampling brambles,
Waving his gun like a paddle.

I thought I'd brushed with a neighbour –
Fox-reek, a warm web, rich as creosote,
Draping the last watery blackberries –
But it was the funeral service.

Two nights he has lain, patient in his position,
Puckered under the first dews of being earth,
Crumpled like dead bracken. His reek will cling
To his remains till spring.

Then I shall steal his fangs, and wear them, and honour
them.

A Cranefly in September

She is struggling through grass-mesh – not flying,
Her wide-winged, stiff, weightless basket-work of limbs
Rocking, like an antique wain, a top-heavy ceremonial
   cart
Across mountain summits
(Not planing over water, dipping her tail)
But blundering with long strides, long reachings, reelings
And ginger-glistening wings
From collision to collision.
Aimless in no particular direction,
Just exerting her last to escape out of the overwhelming
Of whatever it is, legs, grass,
The garden, the county, the country, the world –

Sometimes she rests long minutes in the grass forest
Like a fairytale hero, only a marvel can help her.
She cannot fathom the mystery of this forest
In which, for instance, this giant watches –
The giant who knows she cannot be helped in any way.

Her jointed bamboo fuselage,
Her lobster shoulders, and her face
Like a pinhead dragon, with its tender moustache,
And the simple colourless church windows of her wings
Will come to an end, in mid-search, quite soon.
Everything about her, every perfected vestment

147

Is already superfluous.
The monstrous excess of her legs and curly feet
Are a problem beyond her.
The calculus of glucose and chitin inadequate
To plot her through the infinities of the stems.

The frayed apple leaves, the grunting raven, the defunct
    tractor
Sunk in nettles, wait with their multiplications
Like other galaxies.
The sky's Northward September procession, the vast soft
    armistice,
Like an Empire on the move,
Abandons her, tinily embattled
With her cumbering limbs and cumbered brain.

from GAUDETE

Collision with the earth has finally come –
How far can I fall?

A kelp, adrift
In my feeding substance

A mountain
Rooted in stone of heaven

A sea
Full of moon-ghost, with mangling waters

Dust on my head
Helpless to fit the pieces of water
A needle of many Norths

Ark of blood
Which is the magic baggage old men open
And find useless, at the great moment of need

Error on error
Perfumed
With a ribbon of fury

*

Once I said lightly
Even if the worst happens
We can't fall off the earth.

And again I said
No matter what fire cooks us
We shall be still in the pan together.

And words twice as stupid.
Truly hell heard me.

She fell into the earth
And I was devoured.

*

This is the maneater's skull.
These brows were the Arc de Triomphe
To the gullet.

The deaf adder of appetite
Coiled under. It spied through these nacelles
Ignorant of death.

And the whole assemblage flowed hungering through
    the long ways.
Its cry
Quieted the valleys.

It was looking for me.

I was looking for you.

You were looking for me.

*

I see the oak's bride in the oak's grasp.

Nuptials among prehistoric insects
The tremulous convulsion
The inching hydra strength
Among frilled lizards
Dropping twigs, and acorns, and leaves.

The oak is in bliss
Its roots
Lift arms that are a supplication
Crippled with stigmata
Like the sea-carved cliffs earth lifts

Loaded with dumb, uttering effigies
The oak seems to die and to be dead
In its love-act.

As I lie under it

In a brown leaf nostalgia

An acorn stupor.

＊

A primrose petal's edge
Cuts the vision like laser.

And the eye of a hare
Strips the interrogator naked
Of all but some skin of terror –
A starry frost.

Who is this?
She reveals herself, and is veiled.
Somebody

Something grips by the nape
And bangs the brow, as against a wall
Against the untouchable veils

Of the hole which is bottomless

Till blood drips from the mouth.

＊

Waving goodbye, from your banked hospital bed,
Waving, weeping, smiling, flushed
It happened
You knocked the world off, like a flower-vase.

It was the third time. And it smashed.

I turned
I bowed

151

In the morgue I kissed
Your temple's refrigerated glazed
As rained-on graveyard marble, my
Lips queasy, heart non-existent

And straightened
Into sun-darkness

Like a pillar over Athens

Defunct

In the blinding metropolis of cameras.

*

The swallow – rebuilding –
Collects the lot
From the sow's wallow.

But what I did only shifted the dust about.
And what crossed my mind
Crossed into outer space.

And for all rumours of me read obituary
What there truly remains of me
Is that very thing – my absence.

So how will you gather me?

I saw my keeper
Sitting in the sun –

If you can catch that, you are the falcon of falcons.

*

The grass-blade is not without
The loyalty that never was beheld.

And the blackbird
Sleeking from common anything and worm-dirt

Balances a precarious banner
Gold on black, terror and exultation.

The grim badger with armorial mask
Biting spade-steel, teeth and jaw-strake shattered,
Draws that final shuddering battle cry
Out of its backbone.

Me too,
Let me be one of your warriors.

Let your home
Be my home. Your people
My people.

*

I know well
You are not infallible

I know how your huge your unmanageable
Mass of bronze hair shrank to a twist
As thin as a silk scarf, on your skull,
And how your pony's eye darkened larger

Holding too lucidly the deep glimpse
After the humane killer

And I had to lift your hand for you

While your chin sank to your chest
With the sheer weariness
Of taking away from everybody
Your envied beauty, your much-desired beauty

Your hardly-used beauty

Of lifting away yourself
From yourself

And weeping with the ache of the effort

*

Sometimes it comes, a gloomy flap of lightning,
Like the flushed gossip
With the tale that kills

Sometimes it strengthens very slowly
What is already here –
A tree darkening the house.

The saviour
From these veils of wrinkle and shawls of ache

Like the sun
Which is itself cloudless and leafless

Was always here, is always as she was.

*

Calves harshly parted from their mamas
Stumble through all the hedges in the country
Hither thither crying day and night
Till their throats will only grunt and whistle.

After some days, a stupor sadness
Collects them again in their field.
They will never stray any more.
From now on, they only want each other.

So much for calves.
As for the tiger
He lies still
Like left luggage.

He is roaming the earth light, unseen.

He is safe.

Heaven and hell have both adopted him.

*

A bang – a burning –
I opened my eyes
In a vale crumbling with echoes.

A solitary dove
Cries in the tree – I cannot bear it.

From this centre
It wearies the compass.

Am I killed?
Or am I searching?

Is this the rainbow silking my body?

Which wings are these?

*

At the bottom of the Arctic sea, they say.

Or 'Terrible as an army with banners'.

If I wait, I am a castle
Built with blocks of pain.

If I set out
A kayak stitched with pain

*

Your tree – your oak
A glare

Of black upward lightning, a wriggling grab
Momentary
Under the crumbling of stars.

A guard, a dancer
At the pure well of leaf.

Agony in the garden. Annunciation
Of clay, water and the sunlight.
They thunder under its roof.
Its agony is its temple.

Waist-deep, the black oak is dancing
And my eyes pause
On the centuries of its instant
As gnats
Try to winter in its wrinkles.

> The seas are thirsting
> Towards the oak.
>
> The oak is flying
> Astride the earth.

Football at Slack

Between plunging valleys, on a bareback of hill
Men in bunting colours
Bounced, and their blown ball bounced.

The blown ball jumped, and the merry-coloured men
Spouted like water to head it.
The ball blew away downwind –

The rubbery men bounced after it.
The ball jumped up and out and hung on the wind
Over a gulf of treetops.
Then they all shouted together, and the ball blew back.

Winds from fiery holes in heaven
Piled the hills darkening around them
To awe them. The glare light
Mixed its mad oils and threw glooms.
Then the rain lowered a steel press.

Hair plastered, they all just trod water
To puddle glitter. And their shouts bobbed up
Coming fine and thin, washed and happy

While the humped world sank foundering
And the valleys blued unthinkable
Under depth of Atlantic depression –

But the wingers leapt, they bicycled in air
And the goalie flew horizontal

And once again a golden holocaust
Lifted the cloud's edge, to watch them.

Stanbury Moor

These grasses of light
Which think they are alone in the world

These stones of darkness
Which have a world to themselves

This water of light and darkness
Which hardly savours Creation

And this wind
Which has enough just to exist

Are not

A poor family huddled at a poor gleam

Or words in any phrase

Or wolf-beings in a hungry waiting

Or neighbours in a constellation

They are
The armour of bric-à-brac
To which your soul's caddis
Clings with all its courage.

Leaf Mould

In Hardcastle Crags, that echoey museum,
Where she dug leaf mould for her handfuls of garden
And taught you to walk, others are making poems,

Between finger and thumb roll a pine-needle.
Feel the chamfer, feel how they threaded
The sewing machines.

                        And
Billy Holt invented a new shuttle
As like an ant's egg, with its folded worker,
As every other.
You might see an ant carrying one.
                        And
The cordite conscripts tramped away. But the cenotaphs
Of all the shells that got their heads blown off
And their insides blown out
Are these beech-bole stalwarts.
                        And oak, birch,
Holly, sycamore, pine.
                        The lightest air-stir
Released their love-whispers when she walked
The needles weeping, singing, dedicating
Your spectre-double, still in her womb,
To this temple of her *Missa Solemnis*.

White-faced, brain-washed by her nostalgias,
You were her step-up transformer.
She grieved for her girlhood and the fallen.
You mourned for Paradise and its fable.

Giving you the kiss of life
She hung round your neck her whole valley
Like David's harp.
Now, whenever you touch it, God listens
Only for her voice.

Leaf mould. Blood-warm. Fibres crumbled alive
Between thumb and finger.
Feel again
The clogs twanging your footsoles, on the street's steepness,
As you escaped.

Moors

Are a stage
For the performance of heaven.
Any audience is incidental.

A chess-world of top-heavy Kings and Queens
Circling in stilted majesty
Tremble the bog-cotton
Under the sweep of their robes.

Fools in sunny motley tumble across,
A laughter – fading in full view
To grass-tips tapping at stones.

The witch-brew boiling in the sky-vat
Spins electrical terrors
In the eyes of sheep.

Fleeing wraith-lovers twist and collapse
In death-pact languor
To bedew harebells
On the spoil-heaps of quarries.

Wounded champions lurch out of sunset
To gurgle their last gleams into potholes.

Shattered, bowed armies, huddling leaderless
Escape from a world
Where snipe work late.

Chinese History of Colden Water

A fallen immortal found this valley –
Leafy conch of whispers
On the shore of heaven. He brought to his ear
The mad singing in the hills,
The prophetic mouth of the rain –

These hushings lulled him. So he missed
The goblins toiling up the brook.
The clink of fairy hammers forged his slumber
To a migraine of headscarves and clatter
Of clog-irons and looms and gutter water
And clog-irons and biblical texts.

Till he woke in a terror, tore free, lay panting.
The dream streamed from him. He blinked away
The bloody matter of the Cross
And the death's-head after-image of 'Poor'.

Chapels, chimneys, roofs in the mist – scattered.

Hills with raised wings were standing on hills.
They rode the waves of light
That rocked the conch of whispers

And washed and washed at his eye.
                                        Washed from his ear

All but the laughter of foxes.

Rhododendrons

Dripped a chill virulence
Into my nape –
Rubberized prison-wear of suppression!

Guarding and guarded by
The Council's black
Forbidding forbidden stones.

The policeman's protected leaf!

Detestable evergreen sterility!
Over dead acid gardens
Where blue widows, shrined in Sunday, shrank

To arthritic clockwork,
Yapped like terriers and shook sticks from doorways
Vast and black and proper as museums.

Cenotaphs and the moor-silence!
Rhododendrons and rain!
It is all one. It is over.

Evergloom of official titivation –
Uniform at the reservoir, and the chapel,
And the graveyard park,

Ugly as a brass-band in India.

Sunstruck

The freedom of Saturday afternoons
Starched to cricket dazzle, nagged at a theorem –
Shaggy valley parapets
Pending like thunder, narrowing the spin-bowler's angle.

The click, disconnected, might have escaped –
A six! And the ball slammed flat!
And the bat in flinders! The heart soaring!
And everybody jumping up and running –

Fleeing after the ball, stampeding
Through the sudden hole in Saturday – but
Already clapped into hands and the trap-shout
The ball jerked back to the stumper on its elastic.

Everything collapsed that bit deeper
Towards Monday.

Misery of the brassy sycamores!
Misery of the swans and the hard ripple!

Then again Yes Yes a wild YES –
The bat flashed round the neck in a tight coil,

The stretched shout snatching for the North Sea –
But it fell far short, even of Midgley.

And the legs running for dear life, twinkling white
In the cage of wickets
Were cornered again by the ball, pinned to the crease,
Blocked by the green and white pavilion.

Cross-eyed, mid-stump, sun-descending headache!
Brain sewn into the ball's hide
Hammering at four corners of abstraction
And caught and flung back, and caught, and again
    caught

To be bounced on baked earth, to be clubbed
Toward the wage-mirage sparkle of mills
Toward Lord Savile's heather
Toward the veto of the poisonous Calder

Till the eyes, glad of anything, dropped
From the bails
Into the bottom of a teacup,
To sandwich crusts for the canal cygnets.

The bowler had flogged himself to a dishclout.
And the burned batsmen returned, with changed faces,
'Like men returned from a far journey',
Under the long glare walls of evening

To the cool sheet and the black slot of home.

Curlews

I

They lift
Out of the maternal watery blue lines

Stripped of all but their cry
Some twists of near-inedible sinew

163

They slough off
The robes of bilberry blue
The cloud-stained bogland

They veer up and eddy away over
The stone horns

They trail a long, dangling, falling aim
Across water

Lancing their voices
Through the skin of this light

Drinking the nameless and naked
Through trembling bills.

II

Curlews in April
Hang their harps over the misty valleys

A wobbling water-call
A wet-footed god of the horizons

New moons sink into the heather
And full golden moons

Bulge over spent walls.

For Billy Holt

The longships got this far. Then
Anchored in nose and chin.

Badlands where outcast and outlaw
Fortified the hill-knowle's long outlook.

A far, veiled gaze of quietly
Homicidal appraisal.

Mount Zion

Blackness
Was a building blocking the moon.
Its wall – my first world-direction –
Mount Zion's gravestone slab.

Above the kitchen window, that uplifted mass
Was a deadfall –
Darkening the sun of every day
Right to the eleventh hour.

Marched in under, gripped by elders
Like a jibbing calf
I knew what was coming.
The convicting holy eyes, the convulsed Moses
  mouthings –
Mouths that God had burnt with the breath of Moriah.
They were terrified too.
A mesmerized commissariat,
They terrified me, but they terrified each other.
And Christ was only a naked bleeding worm
Who had given up the ghost.

Women bleak as Sunday rose-gardens
Or crumpling to puff-pastry, and cobwebbed with
  deaths.
Men in their prison-yard, at attention,
Exercising their cowed, shaven souls.
Lips stretching saliva, eyes fixed like the eyes
Of cockerels hung by the legs,
As the bottomless cry
Beat itself numb again against Wesley's foundation
  stone.

Warm shouts at dusk!
A cricket had rigged up its music
In a crack of Mount Zion wall.

A poverty
That cut rock lumps for words.

Requisitioned rain, then more rain,
For walls and roof.

Enfolding arms of sour hills
For company.

Blood in the veins
For amusement.

A graveyard
For homeland.

When Men Got to the Summit

Light words forsook them.
They filled with heavy silence.

Houses came to support them,
But the hard, foursquare scriptures fractured
And the cracks filled with soft rheumatism.

Streets bent to the task
Of holding it all up
Bracing themselves, taking the strain
Till their vertebrae slipped.

The hills went on gently
Shaking their sieve.

Nevertheless, for some giddy moments
A television
Blinked from the wolf's lookout.

The Canal's Drowning Black

Bred wild leopards – among the pale depth fungus.
Loach. Torpid, ginger-bearded, secret
Prehistory of the canal's masonry,
With little cupid mouths.

Five inches huge!
On the slime-brink, over bridge reflections,
I teetered. Then a ringing, skull-jolt stamp
And their beards flowered sudden anemones

All down the sunken cliff. A mad-house thrill –
The stonework's tiny eyes, two feet, three feet,
Four feet down through my reflection
Watched for my next move.

Their schooldays were over.
Peeping man was no part of their knowledge.
So when a monkey god, a Martian
Tickled their underchins with his net rim

They snaked out and over the net rim easy
Back into the oligocene –
Only restrained by a mesh of kitchen curtain.
Then flopped out of their ocean-shifting aeons

Into a two-pound jam-jar
On a windowsill
Blackened with acid rain fall-out
From Manchester's rotten lung.

Next morning, Mount Zion's
Cowled, Satanic majesty behind me
I lobbed – one by one – high through the air
The stiff, pouting, failed, paled new moons

Back into their Paradise and mine.

Cock-Crows

I stood on a dark summit, among dark summits –
Tidal dawn was splitting heaven from earth,
The oyster
Opening to taste gold.

And I heard the cock-crows kindling in the valley
Under the mist –
They were sleepy,
Bubbling deep in the valley cauldron.

Then one or two tossed clear, like soft rockets
And sank back again dimming.

Then soaring harder, brighter, higher
Tearing the mist,
Bubble-glistenings flung up and bursting to light
Brightening the undercloud,
The fire-crests of the cocks – the sickle shouts,
Challenge against challenge, answer to answer,
Hooking higher,
Clambering up the sky as they melted,
Hanging smouldering from the night's fringes.

Till the whole valley brimmed with cock-crows
A magical soft mixture boiling over,
Spilling and sparkling into other valleys

Lobbed-up horse-shoes of glow-swollen metal
From sheds in back-gardens, hen-cotes, farms
Sinking back mistily

Till the last spark died, and embers paled

And the sun climbed into its wet sack
For the day's work

While the dark rims hardened
Over the smoke of towns, from holes in earth

A cricket! The news awful, the shouts awful, at dusk –
Like the bear-alarm, at dusk, among smoky tents –
What was a cricket? How big is a cricket?

Long after I'd been smothered in bed
I could hear them
Riving at the religious stonework
With their furious chisels and screwdrivers.

The Long Tunnel Ceiling

Of the main-road canal bridge
Cradled black stalactite reflections.
That was the place for dark loach!

At the far end, the Moderna blanket factory
And the bushy mask of Hathershelf above it
Peered in through the cell-window.

Lorries from Bradford, baled with plump and towering
Wools and cottons met, above my head,
Lorries from Rochdale, and ground past each other
Making that cavern of air and water tremble –

Suddenly a crash!
The long gleam-ponderous watery echo shattered.

And at last it had begun!
That could only have been a brick from the ceiling!
The bridge was starting to collapse!

But the canal swallowed its scare,
The heavy mirror reglassed itself,
And the black arch gazed up at the black arch.

Till a brick
Rose through its eruption – hung massive
Then slammed back with a shock and a shattering.

An ingot!
Holy of holies! A treasure!
A trout
Nearly as long as my arm, solid
Molten pig of many a bronze loach!

There he lay – lazy – a free lord,
Ignoring me. Caressing, dismissing
The eastward easing traffic of drift,
Master of the Pennine Pass!

Found in some thin glitter among mean gritstone,
High under ferns, high up near sour heather,

Brought down on a midnight cloudburst
In a shake-up of heaven and the hills
When the streams burst with zig-zags and explosions

A seed
Of the wild god now flowering for me
Such a tigerish, dark, breathing lily
Between the tyres, under the tortured axles.

Tree

A priest from a different land
Fulminated
Against heather, black stones, blown water.

Excommunicated the clouds
Damned the wind
Cast the bog pools into outer darkness
Smote the horizons
With the jawbone of emptiness

Till he ran out of breath –

In that teetering moment
Of lungs empty
When only his eye-water protected him
He saw
Heaven and earth moving.

And words left him.
Mind left him. God left him.

Bowed –
The lightning conductor
Of a maiming glimpse – the new prophet –

Under unending interrogation by wind
Tortured by huge scaldings of light
Tried to confess all but could not
Bleed a word

Stripped to his root-letter, cruciform
Contorted
Tried to tell all

Through crooking of elbows
Twitching of finger-ends.

Finally
Resigned
To be dumb.

Lets what happens to him simply happen.

Heptonstall Old Church

A great bird landed here.

Its song drew men out of rock,
Living men out of bog and heather.

Its song put a light in the valleys
And harness on the long moors.

Its song brought a crystal from space
And set it in men's heads.

Then the bird died.

Its giant bones
Blackened and became a mystery.

The crystal in men's heads
Blackened and fell to pieces.

The valleys went out.
The moorland broke loose.

Widdop

Where there was nothing
Somebody put a frightened lake.

Where there was nothing
Stony shoulders
Broadened to support it.

A wind from between the stars
Swam down to sniff at the trembling.

Trees, holding hands, eyes closed,
Acted at world.

Some heath-grass crept close, in fear.

Nothing else
Except when a gull blows through

A rip on the fabric

Out of nothingness into nothingness

Emily Brontë

The wind on Crow Hill was her darling.
His fierce, high tale in her ear was her secret.
But his kiss was fatal.

Through her dark Paradise ran
The stream she loved too well
That bit her breast.

The shaggy sodden king of that kingdom
Followed through the wall
And lay on her love-sick bed.

The curlew trod in her womb.

The stone swelled under her heart.

Her death is a baby-cry on the moor.

Rain

Rain. Floods. Frost. And after frost, rain.
Dull roof-drumming. Wraith-rain pulsing across purple-
     bare woods
Like light across heaved water. Sleet in it.
And the poor fields, miserable tents of their hedges.
Mist-rain off-world. Hills wallowing
In and out of a grey or silvery dissolution. A farm
     gleaming,
Then all dull in the near drumming. At field-corners
Brown water backing and brimming in grass.
Toads hop across rain-hammered roads. Every mutilated
     leaf there
Looks like a frog or a rained-out mouse. Cattle
Wait under blackened backs. We drive post-holes.
They half fill with water before the post goes in.
Mud-water spurts as the iron bar slam-burns
The oak stake-head dry. Cows
Tamed on the waste mudded like a rugby field
Stand and watch, come very close for company
In the rain that goes on and on, and gets colder.
They sniff the wire, sniff the tractor, watch. The hedges
Are straggles of gap. A few haws. Every half-ton cow
Sinks to the fetlock at every sliding stride.
They are ruining their field and they know it.
They look out sideways from under their brows which
     are
Their only shelter. The sunk scrubby wood
Is a pulverized wreck, rain riddles its holes
To the drowned roots. A pheasant looking black
In his waterproofs, bends at his job in the stubble.

The mid-afternoon dusk soaks into
The soaked thickets. Nothing protects them.
The fox corpses lie beaten to their bare bones,
Skin beaten off, brains and bowels beaten out.
Nothing but their blueprint bones last in the rain,
Sodden soft. Round their hay racks, calves
Stand in a shine of mud. The gateways
Are deep obstacles of mud. The calves look up, through
    plastered forelocks,
Without moving. Nowhere they can go
Is less uncomfortable. The brimming world
And the pouring sky are the only places
For them to be. Fieldfares squeal over, sodden
Toward the sodden wood. A raven,
Cursing monotonously, goes over fast
And vanishes in rain-mist. Magpies
Shake themselves hopelessly, hop in the spatter. Misery.
Surviving green of ferns and brambles is tumbled
Like an abandoned scrapyard. The calves
Wait deep beneath their spines. Cows roar
Then hang their noses to the mud.
Snipe go over, invisible in the dusk,
With their squelching cries.

4 December 1973

Dehorning

Bad-tempered bullying bunch, the horned cows
Among the unhorned. Feared, spoilt.
Cantankerous at the hay, at assemblies, at crowded
Yard operations. Knowing their horn-tips' position
To a fraction, every other cow knowing it too.
Like their own tenderness. Horning of bellies, hair-
    tufting

Of horn-tips. Handy levers. But
Off with the horns.
So there they all are in the yard –
The pick of the bullies, churning each other
Like thick fish in a bucket, churning their mud.
One by one, into the cage of the crush: the needle,
A roar not like a cow – more like a tiger,
Blast of air down a cavern, and long, long
Beginning in pain and ending in terror – then the next.
The needle between the horn and the eye, so deep
Your gut squirms for the eyeball twisting
In its pink-white fastenings of tissue. This side and that.
Then the first one anaesthetized, back in the crush.
The bulldog pincers in the septum, stretched full
        strength,
The horn levered right over, the chin pulled round
With the pincers, the mouth drooling, the eye
Like a live eye caught in a pan, like the eye of a fish
Imprisoned in air. Then the cheese cutter
Of braided wire, and stainless steel peg handles,
Aligned on the hair-bedded root of the horn, then
        leaning
Backward full weight, pull-punching backwards,
Left right left right and the blood leaks
Down over the cheekbone, the wire bites
And buzzes, the ammonia horn-burn smokes
And the cow groans, roars shapelessly, hurls
Its half-ton commotion in the tight cage. Our faces
Grimace like faces in the dentist's chair. The horn
Rocks from its roots, the wire pulls through
The last hinge of hair, the horn is heavy and free,
And a water-pistol jet of blood
Rains over the one who holds it – a needle jet
From the white-rasped and bloody skull-crater. Then
        tweezers
Twiddle the artery nozzle, knotting it enough,

And purple antiseptic squirts a cuttlefish cloud over it.
Then the other side the same. We collect
A heap of horns. The floor of the crush
Is a trampled puddle of scarlet. The purple-crowned
    cattle,
The bullies, with suddenly no horns to fear,
Start ramming and wrestling. Maybe their heads
Are still anaesthetized. A new order
Among the hornless. The bitchy high-headed
Straight-back brindle, with her Spanish bull trot,
And her head-shaking snorting advance and her crazy
    spirit,
Will have to get maternal. What she's lost
In weapons, she'll have to make up for in tits.
But they've all lost one third of their beauty.

14 May 1974

Bringing in New Couples

Wind out of freezing Europe. A mean snow
Fiery cold. Ewes caked crusty with snow,
Their new hot lambs wet trembling
And crying on trampled patches, under the hedge –
Twenty miles of open lower landscape
Blows into their wetness. The field smokes and writhes
Burning like a moor with snow-fumes.
Lambs nestling to make themselves comfortable
While the ewe nudges and nibbles at them
And the numbing snow-wind blows on the blood tatters
At her breached back-end.
The moor a grey sea-shape. The wood
Thick-fingered density, a worked wall of whiteness.
The old sea-roar, sheep-shout, lamb-wail.
Redwings needling invisible. A fright

Smoking among trees, the hedges blocked.
Lifting of ice-heavy ewes, trampling anxieties
As they follow their wide-legged tall lambs,
Tripods craning to cry bewildered.
We coax the mothers to follow their babies
And they do follow, running back
In sudden convinced panic to the patch
Where the lamb had been born, dreading
She must have been deceived away from it
By crafty wolvish humans, then coming again
Defenceless to the bleat she's attuned to
And recognizing her own – a familiar
Detail in the meaningless shape-mass
Of human arms, legs, body-clothes – her lamb on the
    white earth
Held by those hands. Then vanishing again
Lifted. Then only the disembodied cry
Going with the human, while she runs in a circle
On the leash of the cry. While the wind
Presses outer space into the grass
And alarms wrens deep in brambles
With hissing fragments of stars.

16 February 1975

Tractor

The tractor stands frozen – an agony
To think of. All night
Snow packed its open entrails. Now a head-pincering
    gale,
A spill of molten ice, smoking snow,
Pours into its steel.
At white heat of numbness it stands
In the aimed hosing of ground-level fieriness.

179

It defies flesh and won't start.
Hands are like wounds already
Inside armour gloves, and feet are unbelievable
As if the toe-nails were all just torn off.
I stare at it in hatred. Beyond it
The copse hisses – capitulates miserably
In the fleeing, failing light. Starlings,
A dirtier sleetier snow, blow smokily, unendingly, over
Towards plantations eastward.
All the time the tractor is sinking
Through the degrees, deepening
Into its hell of ice.

The starter lever
Cracks its action, like a snapping knuckle.
The battery is alive – but like a lamb
Trying to nudge its solid-frozen mother –
While the seat claims my buttock-bones, bites
With the space-cold of earth, which it has joined
In one solid lump.

I squirt commercial sure-fire
Down the black throat – it just coughs.
It ridicules me – a trap of iron stupidity
I've stepped into. I drive the battery
As if I were hammering and hammering
The frozen arrangement to pieces with a hammer
And it jabbers laughing pain-crying mockingly
Into happy life.

And stands
Shuddering itself full of heat, seeming to enlarge slowly
Like a demon demonstrating
A more-than-usually-complete materialization –
Suddenly it jerks from its solidarity
With the concrete, and lurches towards a stanchion
Bursting with superhuman well-being and abandon
Shouting Where Where?

Worse iron is waiting. Power-lift kneels,
Levers awake imprisoned deadweight,
Shackle-pins bedded in cast-iron cow-shit.
The blind and vibrating condemned obedience
Of iron to the cruelty of iron,
Wheels screeched out of their night-locks –

Fingers
Among the tormented
Tonnage and burning of iron

Eyes
Weeping in the wind of chloroform

And the tractor, streaming with sweat,
Raging and trembling and rejoicing.

31 January 1976

Roe-Deer

In the dawn-dirty light, in the biggest snow of the year
Two blue-dark deer stood in the road, alerted.

They had happened into my dimension
The moment I was arriving just there.

They planted their two or three years of secret deerhood
Clear on my snow-screen vision of the abnormal

And hesitated in the all-way disintegration
And stared at me. And so for some lasting seconds

I could think the deer were waiting for me
To remember the password and sign

That the curtain had blown aside for a moment
And there where the trees were no longer trees, nor the
    road a road

The deer had come for me.

Then they ducked through the hedge, and upright they
    rode their legs
Away downhill over a snow-lonely field

Towards tree dark – finally
Seeming to eddy and glide and fly away up

Into the boil of big flakes.
The snow took them and soon their nearby hoofprints as
    well

Revising its dawn inspiration
Back to the ordinary.

13 February 1973

Sketching a Thatcher

Bird-bones is on the roof. Seventy-eight
And still a ladder squirrel,
Three or four nitches at a time, up forty rungs,
Then crabbing out across the traverse,
Cock-crows of insulting banter, liberated
Into his old age, like a royal fool
But still tortured with energy. Thatching
Must be the sinless job. Weathered
Like a weathercock, face bright as a ploughshare,
Skinny forearms of steely cable, batting
The reeds flush, crawling, cliff-hanging,
Lizard-silk of his lizard-skinny hands,
Hands never still, twist of body never still –
Bounds in for a cup of tea, 'Caught you all asleep!'
Markets all the gossip – cynical old goblin
Cackling with wicked joy. Bounds out –
Trips and goes full length, bounces back upright,

'Haven't got the weight to get hurt with!' Cheers
Every departure – 'Off for a drink?' and 'Off
To see his fancy woman again!' – leans from the sky,
Sun-burned-out pale eyes, eyes bleached
As old thatch, in the worn tool of his face,
In his haggard pants and his tired-out shirt –
They can't keep up with him. He just can't
Stop working. 'I don't want the money!' He'd
Prefer a few years. 'Have to sell the house to pay me!'
Alertness built into the bird-stare,
The hook of his nose, bill-hook of his face.
Suns have worn him, like an old sun-tool
Of the day-making, an old shoe-tongue
Of the travelling weathers, the hand-palm, ageless,
Of all winds on all roofs. He lams the roof
And the house quakes. Was everybody
Once like him? He's squirmed through
Some tight cranny of natural selection.
The nut-stick yealm-twist's got into his soul,
He didn't break. He's proof
As his crusty roofs. He ladder-dances
His blood light as spirit. His muscles
Must be clean as horn.
And the whole house
Is more pleased with itself, him on it,
Cresting it, and grooming it, and slapping it
Than if an eagle rested there. Sitting
Drinking his tea, he looks like a tatty old eagle,
And his yelping laugh of derision
Is just like a tatty old eagle's.

Ravens

As we came through the gate to look at the few new
  lambs
On the skyline of lawn smoothness,
A raven bundled itself into air from midfield
And slid away under hard glistenings, low and guilty.
Sheep nibbling, kneeling to nibble the reluctant nibbled
  grass.
Sheep staring, their jaws pausing to think, then chewing
  again,
Then pausing. Over there a new lamb
Just getting up, bumping its mother's nose
As she nibbles the sugar coating off it
While the tattered banners of her triumph swing and
  drip from her rear-end.
She sneezes and a glim of water flashes from her rear-
  end.
She sneezes again and again, till she's emptied.
She carries on investigating her new present and seeing
  how it works.
Over here is something else. But you are still interested
In that new one, and its new spark of voice,
And its tininess.
Now over here, where the raven was,
Is what interests you next. Born dead,
Twisted like a scarf, a lamb of an hour or two,
Its insides, the various jellies and crimsons and
  transparencies
And threads and tissues pulled out
In straight lines, like tent ropes
From its upward belly opened like a lamb-wool slipper,
The fine anatomy of silvery ribs on display and the
  cavity,
The head also emptied through the eye-sockets,
The woolly limbs swathed in birth-yolk and impossible

To tell now which in all this field of quietly nibbling
    sheep
Was its mother. I explain
That it died being born. We should have been here, to
    help it.
So it died being born. 'And did it cry?' you cry.
I pick up the dangling greasy weight by the hooves soft
    as dogs' pads
That had trodden only womb-water
And its raven-drawn strings dangle and trail,
Its loose head joggles, and 'Did it cry?' you cry again.
Its two-fingered feet splay in their skin between the
    pressures
Of my fingers and thumb. And there is another,
Just born, all black, splaying its tripod, inching its new
    points
Towards its mother, and testing the note
It finds in its mouth. But you have eyes now
Only for the tattered bundle of throwaway lamb.
'Did it cry?' you keep asking, in a three-year-old field-
    wide
Piercing persistence. 'Oh yes' I say 'it cried.'

Though this one was lucky insofar
As it made the attempt into a warm wind
And its first day of death was blue and warm
The magpies gone quiet with domestic happiness
And skylarks not worrying about anything
And the blackthorn budding confidently
And the skyline of hills, after millions of hard years,
Sitting soft.

                                                      15 April 1974

February 17th

A lamb could not get born. Ice wind
Out of a downpour dishclout sunrise. The mother
Lay on the mudded slope. Harried, she got up
And the blackish lump bobbed at her back-end
Under her tail. After some hard galloping,
Some manoeuvring, much flapping of the backward
Lump head of the lamb looking out,
I caught her with a rope. Laid her, head uphill
And examined the lamb. A blood-ball swollen
Tight in its black felt, its mouth gap
Squashed crooked, tongue stuck out, black-purple,
Strangled by its mother. I felt inside,
Past the noose of mother-flesh, into the slippery
Muscled tunnel, fingering for a hoof,
Right back to the port-hole of the pelvis.
But there was no hoof. He had stuck his head out too
     early
And his feet could not follow. He should have
Felt his way, tip-toe, his toes
Tucked up under his nose
For a safe landing. So I kneeled wrestling
With her groans. No hand could squeeze past
The lamb's neck into her interior
To hook a knee. I roped that baby head
And hauled till she cried out and tried
To get up and I saw it was useless. I went
Two miles for the injection and a razor.
Sliced the lamb's throat-strings, levered with a knife
Between the vertebrae and brought the head off
To stare at its mother, its pipes sitting in the mud
With all earth for a body. Then pushed
The neck-stump right back in, and as I pushed
She pushed. She pushed crying and I pushed gasping.
And the strength

Of the birth push and the push of my thumb
Against that wobbly vertebra were deadlock,
A to-fro futility. Till I forced
A hand past and got a knee. Then like
Pulling myself to the ceiling with one finger
Hooked in a loop, timing my effort
To her birth push groans, I pulled against
The corpse that would not come. Till it came.
And after it the long, sudden, yolk-yellow
Parcel of life
In a smoking slither of oils and soups and syrups –
And the body lay born, beside the hacked-off head.

17 February 1974

Birth of Rainbow

This morning blue vast clarity of March sky
But a blustery violence of air, and a soaked overnight
Newpainted look to the world. The wind coming
Off the snowed moor in the South, razorish
Heavy-bladed and head-cutting, off snow-powdered
    ridges.
Flooded ruts shook. Hoof-puddles flashed. A daisy
Mud-plastered unmixed its head from the mud.
The black and white cow, on the highest crest of the
    round ridge,
Stood under the end of a rainbow.
Head down licking something, full in the painful wind
That the pouring haze of the rainbow ignored.
She was licking her gawky black calf
Collapsed wet-fresh from the womb, blinking his eyes
In the low morning dazzling washed sun.
Black, wet as a collie from a river, as she licked him,
Finding his smells, learning his particularity.

A flag of bloody tissue hung from her back-end
Spreading and shining, pink-fleshed and raw, it flapped
  and coiled
In the unsparing wind. She positioned herself, uneasy
As we approached, nervous small footwork
On the hoof-ploughed drowned sod of the ruined field.
She made uneasy low noises, and her calf too
With his staring whites, mooed the full clear calf-note
Pure as woodwind, and tried to get up,
Tried to get his cantilever front legs
In operation, lifted his shoulders, hoisted to his knees,
Then hoisted his back-end and lurched forward
On his knees and crumpling ankles, sliding in the mud
And collapsing plastered. She went on licking him.
She started eating the banner of thin raw flesh that
Spinnakered from her rear. We left her to it.
Blobbed antiseptic on to the sodden blood-dangle
Of his muddy birth-cord, and left her
Inspecting the new smell. The whole South West
Was black as nightfall.
Trailing squall-smokes hung over the moor leaning
And whitening towards us, then the world blurred
And disappeared in forty-five degree hail
And a gate-jerking blast. We got to cover.
Left to God the calf and his mother.

19 March 1974

Coming Down Through Somerset

I flash-glimpsed in the headlights – the high moment
Of driving through England – a killed badger
Sprawled with helpless legs. Yet again
Manoeuvred lane-ends, retracked, waited
Out of decency for headlights to die,

Lifted by one warm hindleg in the world-night
A slain badger. August dust-heat. Beautiful,
Beautiful, warm, secret beast. Bedded him
Passenger, bleeding from the nose. Brought him close
Into my life. Now he lies on the beam
Torn from a great building. Beam waiting two years
To be built into new building. Summer coat
Not worth skinning off him. His skeleton – for the
    future.
Fangs, handsome concealed. Flies, drumming,
Bejewel his transit. Heatwave ushers him hourly
Towards his underworlds. A grim day of flies
And sunbathing. Get rid of that badger.
A night of shrunk rivers, glowing pastures,
Sea-trout shouldering up through trickles. Then the sun
    again
Waking like a torn-out eye. How strangely
He stays on into the dawn – how quiet
The dark bear-claws, the long frost-tipped guard hairs!
Get rid of that badger today.
And already the flies.
More passionate, bringing their friends. I don't want
To bury and waste him. Or skin him (it is too late).
Or hack off his head and boil it
To liberate his masterpiece skull. I want him
To stay as he is. Sooty gloss-throated,
With his perfect face. Paws so tired,
Power-body relegated. I want him
To stop time. His strength staying, bulky,
Blocking time. His rankness, his bristling wildness,
His thrillingly painted face.
A badger on my moment of life.
Not years ago, like the others, but now.
I stand
Watching his stillness, like an iron nail

Driven, flush to the head,
Into a yew post. Something has to stay.

8 August 1975

The Day He Died

Was the silkiest day of the young year,
The first reconnaissance of the real spring,
The first confidence of the sun.

That was yesterday. Last night, frost.
And as hard as any of all winter.
Mars and Saturn and the Moon dangling in a bunch
On the hard, littered sky.
Today is Valentine's day.

Earth toast-crisp. The snowdrops battered.
Thrushes spluttering. Pigeons gingerly
Rubbing their voices together, in stinging cold.
Crows creaking, and clumsily
Cracking loose.

The bright fields look dazed.
Their expression is changed.
They have been somewhere awful
And come back without him.

The trustful cattle, with frost on their backs,
Waiting for hay, waiting for warmth,
Stand in a new emptiness.

From now on the land
Will have to manage without him.
But it hesitates, in this slow realization of light,
Childlike, too naked, in a frail sun,
With roots cut
And a great blank in its memory.

A Memory

Your bony white bowed back, in a singlet,
Powerful as a horse,
Bowed over an upturned sheep
Shearing under the East chill through-door draught
In the cave-dark barn, sweating and freezing –
Flame-crimson face, drum-guttural African curses
As you bundled the sheep
Like tying some oversize, overweight, spilling bale
Through its adjustments of position

The attached cigarette, bent at its glow
Preserving its pride of ash
Through all your suddenly savage, suddenly gentle
Masterings of the animal

You were like a collier, a face-worker
In a dark hole of obstacle
Heedless of your own surfaces
Inching by main strength into the solid hour,
Bald, arch-wrinkled, weathered dome bowed
Over your cigarette comfort

Till you stretched erect through a groan
Letting a peeled sheep leap free

Then nipped the bud of stub from your lips
And with glove-huge, grease-glistening carefulness
Lit another at it

from EARTH-NUMB

Earth-Numb

Dawn – a smouldering fume of dry frost.
Sky-edge of red-hot iron.
Daffodils motionless – some fizzled out.
The birds – earth-brim simmering.
Sycamore buds unsticking – the leaf out-crumpling,
    purplish.

The pheasant cock's glare-cry. Jupiter ruffling softly.

Hunting salmon. And hunted
And haunted by apparitions from tombs
Under the smoothing tons of dead element
In the river's black canyons.

The lure is a prayer. And my searching –
Like the slow sun.
A prayer, like a flower opening.
A surgeon operating
On an open heart, with needles –

And bang! the river grabs at me

A mouth-flash, an electrocuting malice
Like a trap, trying to rip life off me –
And the river stiffens alive,
The black hole thumps, the whole river hauls
And I have one.

A piling voltage hums, jamming me stiff –
Something terrified and terrifying
Gleam-surges to and fro through me
From the river to the sky, from the sky into the rivei

Uprooting dark bedrock, shatters it in air,
Cartwheels across me, slices thudding through me
As if I were the current –

Till the fright flows all one way down the line

And a ghost grows solid, a hoverer,
A lizard green slither, banner heavy –

Then the wagging stone pebble head
Trying to think on shallows –

Then the steel spectre of purples
From the forge of water
Gagging on emptiness

As the eyes of incredulity
Fix their death-exposure of the celandine and the cloud.

A Motorbike

We had a motorbike all through the war
In an outhouse – thunder, flight, disruption
Cramped in rust, under washing, abashed, outclassed
By the Brens, the Bombs, the Bazookas elsewhere.

The war ended, the explosions stopped.
The men surrendered their weapons
And hung around limply.
Peace took them all prisoner.
They were herded into their home towns.
A horrible privation began
Of working a life up out of the avenues
And the holiday resorts and the dance-halls.

Then the morning bus was as bad as any labour truck,
The foreman, the boss, as bad as the S.S.
And the ends of the street and the bends of the road

And the shallowness of the shops and the shallowness of
    the beer
And the sameness of the next town
Were as bad as electrified barbed wire
The shrunk-back war ached in their testicles
And England dwindled to the size of a dog-track.

So there came this quiet young man
And he bought our motorbike for twelve pounds.
And he got it going, with difficulty.
He kicked it into life – it erupted
Out of the six-year sleep, and he was delighted.

A week later, astride it, before dawn,
A misty frosty morning,
He escaped

Into a telegraph pole
On the long straight west of Swinton.

Deaf School

The deaf children were monkey-nimble, fish-tremulous
    and sudden.
Their faces were alert and simple
Like faces of little animals, small night lemurs caught in
    the flash-light.
They lacked a dimension,
They lacked a subtle wavering aura of sound and
    responses to sound.
The whole body was removed
From the vibration of air, they lived through the eyes,
The clear simple look, the instant full attention.
Their selves were not woven into a voice
Which was woven into a face
Hearing itself, its own public and audience,

An apparition in camouflage, an assertion in doubt –
Their selves were hidden, and their faces looked out of
    hiding.
What they spoke with was a machine,
A manipulation of fingers, a control-panel of gestures
Out there in the alien space
Separated from them –

Their unused faces were simple lenses of watchfulness
Simple pools of earnest watchfulness

Their bodies were like their hands
Nimbler than bodies, like the hammers of a piano,
A puppet agility, a simple mechanical action
A blankness of hieroglyph
A stylized lettering
Spelling out approximate signals

While the self looked through, out of the face of simple
    concealment
A face not merely deaf, a face in darkness, a face
    unaware,
A face that was simply the front skin of the self
    concealed and separate

Life is Trying to be Life

Death also is trying to be life.
Death is in the sperm like the ancient mariner
With his horrible tale.

Death mews in the blankets – is it a kitten?
It plays with dolls but cannot get interested.
It stares at the windowlight and cannot make it out.
It wears baby clothes and is patient.
It learns to talk, watching the others' mouths.
It laughs and shouts and listens to itself numbly.

It stares at people's faces
And sees their skin like a strange moon, and stares at the
     grass
In its position just as yesterday.
And stares at its fingers and hears: 'Look at that child!'
Death is a changeling
Tortured by daisy chains and Sunday bells
It is dragged about like a broken doll
By little girls playing at mothers and funerals.
Death only wants to be life. It cannot quite manage.

Weeping it is weeping to be life
As for a mother it cannot remember.

Death and Death and Death, it whispers
With eyes closed, trying to feel life

Like the shout in joy
Like the glare in lightning
That empties the lonely oak.
                              And that is the death
In the antlers of the Irish Elk. It is the death
In the cave-wife's needle of bone. Yet it still is not death –

Or in the shark's fang which is a monument
Of its lament
On a headland of life.

Speech out of Shadow

Not your eyes, but what they disguise

Not your skin, with just that texture and light
But what uses it as cosmetic

Not your nose – to be or not to be beautiful
But what it is the spy for

Not your mouth, not your lips, not their adjustments
But the maker of the digestive tract

Not your breasts
Because they are diversion and deferment

Not your sexual parts, your proffered rewards
Which are in the nature of a flower
Technically treacherous

Not the webs of your voice, your poise, your tempo
Your drug of a million micro-signals

But the purpose.

The unearthly stone in the sun.

The glare
Of the falcon, behind its hood

Tamed now
To its own mystifications

And the fingerings of men.

from Seven Dungeon Songs

I

Dead, she became space-earth
Broken to pieces.
Plants nursed her death, unearthed her goodness.

But her murderer, mad-innocent
Sucked at her offspring, reckless of blood,
Consecrating them in fire, muttering
It is good to be God.

He used familiar hands
Incriminating many,

And he borrowed mouths, leaving names
Being himself nothing

But a tiger's sigh, a wolf's music
A song on a lonely road

What it is
Risen out of mud, fallen from space
That stares through a face.

II

Face was necessary – I found face.
Hands – I found hands.

I found shoulders, I found legs
I found all bits and pieces.

We were me, and lay quiet.
I got us all of a piece, and we lay quiet.

We just lay.
Sunlight had prepared a wide place

And we lay there.
Air nursed us.

We recuperated.
While maggots blackened to seeds, and blood warmed its
    stone.

Only still something
Stared at me and screamed

Stood over me, black across the sun,
And mourned me, and would not help me get up.

III

The earth locked out the light,
Blocking the light, like a door locked.
But a crack of light

Between sky and earth, was enough.
He called it, Earth's halo.

And the lizard spread of his fingers
Reached for it.

He called it, The leakage of air
Into this suffocation of earth.

And the gills of his rib-cage
Gulped to get more of it.

His lips pressed to its coolness
Like an eye to a crack.

He lay like the already-dead

Tasting the tears
Of the wind-shaken and weeping
Tree of light.

IV

I walk
Unwind with activity of legs
The tangled ball
Which was once the orderly circuit of my body

Some night in the womb
All my veins and capillaries were taken out
By some evil will
And knotted in a great ball and stuffed back inside me

Now I rush to and fro
I try to attach a raw broken end
To some steady place, then back away
I look for people with clever fingers
Who might undo me

The horrible ball just comes
People's fingers snarl it worse

I hurl myself
To jerk out the knot
Or snap it

And come up short

So dangle and dance
The dance of unbeing

v

If mouth could open its cliff
If ear could unfold from this strata
If eyes could split their rock and peep out finally

If hands of mountain-fold
Could get a proper purchase
If feet of fossil could lift

If head of lakewater and weather
If body of horizon
If whole body and balancing head

If skin of grass could take messages
And do its job properly

If spine of earth-foetus
Could unfurl

If man-shadow out there moved to my moves

The speech that works air
Might speak me

Tiger-Psalm

The tiger kills hungry. The machine-guns
Talk, talk, talk across their Acropolis.
The tiger
Kills expertly, with anaesthetic hand.

The machine-guns
Carry on arguing in heaven
Where numbers have no ears, where there is no blood.
The tiger
Kills frugally, after close inspection of the map.
The machine-guns shake their heads,
They go on chattering statistics.
The tiger kills by thunderbolt:
God of her own salvation.
The machine-guns
Proclaim the Absolute, according to morse,
In a code of bangs and holes that makes men frown.
The tiger
Kills with beautiful colours in her face,
Like a flower painted on a banner.
The machine-guns
Are not interested.
They laugh. They are not interested. They speak and
Their tongues burn soul-blue, haloed with ashes,
Puncturing the illusion.
The tiger
Kills and licks her victim all over carefully.
The machine-guns
Leave a crust of blood hanging on the nails
In an orchard of scrap-iron.
The tiger
Kills
With the strength of five tigers, kills exalted.
The machine-guns
Permit themselves a snigger. They eliminate the error
With a to-fro dialectic
And the point proved stop speaking.
The tiger
Kills like the fall of a cliff, one-sinewed with the earth,
Himalayas under eyelid, Ganges under fur –

Does not kill.

Does not kill. The tiger blesses with a fang.
The tiger does not kill but opens a path
Neither of Life nor of Death:
The tiger within the tiger:
The Tiger of the Earth.
                              O Tiger!
O Sister of the Viper!
                    O Beast in Blossom!

Orts

In the M5 Restaurant

Our sad coats assemble at the counter

The tyre face pasty
The neon of plaster flesh
With little inexplicable eyes
Holding a dish with two buns

Symbolic food
Eaten by symbolic faces
Symbolic eating movements

The road drumming in the wall, drumming in the head

The road going nowhere and everywhere

My freedom evidently
Is to feed my life
Into a carburettor

Petroleum has burned away all
But a still-throbbing column
Of carbon-monoxide and lead.

I attempt a firmer embodiment
With illusory coffee
And a gluey quasi-pie.

That Star

That star
Will blow your hand off
That star
Will scramble your brains and your nerves
That star
Will frazzle your skin off
That star
Will turn everybody yellow and stinking
That star
Will scorch everything dead fumed to its blueprint
That star
Will make the earth melt
That star . . . and so on.

And they surround us. And far into infinity.
These are the armies of the night.
There is no escape.
Not one of them is good, or friendly, or corruptible.

One chance remains: KEEP ON DIGGING THAT HOLE

KEEP ON DIGGING AWAY AT THAT HOLE

Poets

Crowd the horizons, poised, wings
Lifted in elation, vast
Armadas of illusion
Waiting for a puff.

Or they dawn, singing birds – all
Mating calls
Battle bluff
And crazy feathers.

Or disappear
Into the grass-blade atom – one flare
Annihilating the world
To the big-eyed, simple light that fled

When the first word lumped out of the flint.

Grosse Fuge

Rouses in its cave
Under faint peaks of light

Flares abrupt at the sun's edge, dipping again
This side of the disc
Now coming low out of the glare

Coming under skylines
Under seas, under liquid corn
Snaking among poppies

Soft arrival pressing the roof of ghost
Creaking of old foundations
The ear cracking like a dry twig

Heavy craving weight
Of eyes on your nape
Unadjusted to world

Huge inching through hair, through veins
Tightening stealth of blood
Breath in the tunnel of spine

And the maneater
Opens its mouth and the music
Sinks its claw
Into your skull, a single note

Picks you up by the small of the back, weightless
Vaults into space, dangling your limbs

Devours you leisurely among litter of stars
Digests you into its horrible joy
This is the tiger of heaven

Hoists people out of their clothes

Leaves its dark track across the octaves

Children

                              new to the blood
Whose hot push has surpassed
The sabretooth
Never doubt their rights of conquest.

Their voices, under the leaf-dazzle
An occupying army
A foreign tongue
Loud in their idleness and power.

Figures in the flaming of hell
A joy beyond good and evil
Breaking their toys.

Soon they'll sleep where they struck.
They'll leave behind
A man like a licked skull
A gravestone woman, their playthings.

Prospero and Sycorax

She knows, like Ophelia,
The task has swallowed him.
She knows, like George's dragon,
Her screams have closed his helmet.

She knows, like Jocasta,
It is over.
He prefers
Blindness.

She knows, like Cordelia,
He is not himself now,
And what speaks through him must be discounted –
Though it will be the end of them both.

She knows, like God,
He has found
Something
Easier to live with –

His death, and her death.

The Beacon

The Stone

Has not yet been cut.
It is too heavy already
For consideration. Its edges
Are so super-real, already,
And at this distance,
They cut real cuts in the unreal
Stuff of just thinking. So I leave it.
Somewhere it is.
Soon it will come.
I shall not carry it. With horrible life
It will transport its face, with sure strength,
To sit over mine, wherever I look,
Instead of hers.
It will even have across its brow
Her name.

Somewhere it is coming to the end
Of its million million years –
Which have worn her out.
It is coming to the beginning
Of her million million million years
Which will wear out it.

Because she will never move now
Till it is worn out.
She will not move now
Till everything is worn out.

TV Off

He hears lithe trees and last leaves swatting the glass –

Staring into flames, through the grille of age
Like a late fish, face clothed with fungus,
Keeping its mouth upstream.

Remorseful for what nobody any longer suffers
Nostalgic for what he would not give twopence to see
    back
Hopeful for what he will not miss when it fails

Who lay a night and a day and a night and a day
Golden-haired, while his friend beside him
Attending a small hole in his brow
Ripened black.

A God

Pain was pulled down over his eyes like a fool's hat.
They pressed electrodes of pain through the parietals.

He was helpless as a lamb
Which cannot be born
Whose head hangs under its mother's anus.

Pain was stabbed through his palm, at the crutch of the M,
Made of iron, from earth's core.
From that pain he hung,
As if he were being weighed.
The cleverness of his fingers availed him
As the bullock's hooves, in the offal bin,
Avail the severed head
Hanging from its galvanized hook.

Pain was hooked through his foot.
From that pain, too, he hung
As on display.
His patience had meaning only for him
Like the sanguine upside-down grin
Of a hanging half-pig.

There, hanging,
He accepted the pain beneath his ribs
Because he could no more escape it
Than the poulterer's hanging hare,
Hidden behind eyes growing concave,
Can escape
What has replaced its belly.

He could not understand what had happened.

Or what he had become.

Remembering Teheran

How it hung
In the electrical loom
Of the Himalayas – I remember
The spectre of a rose.

All day the flag on the military camp flowed South.

In the Shah's Evin Motel
The Manageress – a thunderhead Atossa –
Wept on her bed
Or struck awe. Tragic Persian
Quaked her bosom – precarious balloons of water –
But still nothing worked.

Everything hung on a prayer, in the hanging dust.

With a splash of keys
She ripped through the lock, filled my room, sulphurous,
With plumbers –
Twelve-year-olds, kneeling to fathom
A pipeless tap sunk in a blank block wall.

*

I had a funny moment
Beside the dried-up river of boulders. A huddle of
    families
Were piling mulberries into wide bowls, under limp,
    dusty trees.
All the big males, in their white shirts,
Drifted out towards me, hands hanging –

I could see the bad connections sparking inside their
   heads

As I picked my way among thistles
Between dead-drop wells – open man-holes
Parched as snake-dens –

Later, three stoned-looking Mercedes,
Splitting with arms and faces, surfed past me
Warily over a bumpy sea of talc,
The uncials on their number-plates like fragments of
   scorpions.

                    *

I imagined all Persia
As a sacred scroll, humbled to powder
By the God-conducting script on it –
The lightning serifs of Zoroaster –
The primal cursive.

                    *

Goats, in charred rags,
Eyes and skulls
Adapted to sunstroke, woke me
Sunbathing among the moon-clinker.
When one of them slowly straightened into a goat-herd
I knew I was in the wrong century
And wrongly dressed.

All around me stood
The tense, abnormal thistles, desert fanatics;
Politicos, in their zinc-blue combat issue;

Three-dimensional crystal theorems
For an optimum impaling of the given air;
Arsenals of pragmatic ideas –

I retreated to the motel terrace, to loll there
And watch the officers half a mile away, exercising their
   obsolete horses.

A bleaching sun, cobalt-cored,
Played with the magnetic field of the mountains.

And prehistoric giant ants, outriders, long-shadowed,
Cast in radiation-proof metals,
Galloped through the land, lightly and unhindered,
Stormed my coffee-saucer, drinking the stain –

At sunset
The army flag rested for a few minutes
Then began to flow North.

              *

I found a living thread of water
Dangling from a pipe. A snake-tongue flicker.
An incognito whisper.
It must have leaked and smuggled itself, somehow,
From the high Mother of Snows, halfway up the sky.
It wriggled these last inches to ease
A garden of pot-pourri, in a tindery shade of peach-
   boughs,
And played there, a fuse crackling softly –

As the whole city
Sank in the muffled drumming
Of a subterranean furnace.

And over it
The desert's bloom of dust, the petroleum smog, the
   transistor commotion
Thickened a pinky-purple thunderlight.

The pollen of the thousands of years of voices
Murmurous, radio-active, rubbing to flash-point --

*

Scintillating through the migraine
The world-authority on Islamic Art
Sipped at a spoonful of yoghurt
And smiling at our smiles described his dancing
Among self-beheaded dancers who went on dancing
    with their heads
(But only God, he said, can create a language).

Journalists proffered, on platters of silence,
Split noses, and sliced-off ears and lips –

*

Chastened, I listened. Then for the belly-dancer
(Who would not dance on my table, would not kiss me
Through her veil, spoke to me only
Through the mouth
Of her demon-mask
Warrior drummer)

I composed a bouquet – a tropic, effulgent
Puff of publicity, in the style of Attar,

And saw myself translated by the drummer
Into her liquid
Lashing shadow, those arabesques of God,

That thorny fount.

Bones

Bones is a crazy pony.
Moon-white – star-mad.
All skull and skeleton.

Her hooves pound. The sleeper awakes with a cry.

Who has broken her in?
Who has mounted her and come back
Or kept her?

She lifts under them, the snaking crest of a bullwhip.

Hero by hero they go –
Grimly get astride
And their hair lifts.

She laughs, smelling the battle – their cry comes back.

Who can live her life?
Every effort to hold her or turn her falls off her
Like rotten harness.

Their smashed faces come back, the wallets and the
    watches.

And this is the stunted foal of the earth –
She that kicks the cot
To flinders and is off.

Do not Pick up the Telephone

That plastic Buddha jars out a Karate screech

Before the soft words with their spores
The cosmetic breath of the gravestone

Death invented the phone it looks like the altar of death
Do not worship the telephone
It drags its worshippers into actual graves
With a variety of devices, through a variety of disguised
    voices

Sit godless when you hear the religious wail of the
    telephone

Do not think your house is a hide-out it is a telephone
Do not think you walk your own road, you walk down a
    telephone
Do not think you sleep in the hand of God you sleep in
    the mouthpiece of a telephone
Do not think your future is yours it waits upon a
    telephone
Do not think your thoughts are your own thoughts they
    are the toys of the telephone
Do not think these days are days they are the sacrificial
    priests of the telephone
The secret police of the telephone

O phone get out of my house
You are a bad god
Go and whisper on some other pillow
Do not lift your snake head in my house
Do not bite any more beautiful people

You plastic crab
Why is your oracle always the same in the end?
What rake-off for you from the cemeteries?

Your silences are as bad
When you are needed, dumb with the malice of the
    clairvoyant insane
The stars whisper together in your breathing
World's emptiness oceans in your mouthpiece
Stupidly your string dangles into the abysses
Plastic you are then stone a broken box of letters
And you cannot utter
Lies or truth, only the evil one
Makes you tremble with sudden appetite to see
    somebody undone

Blackening electrical connections
To where death bleaches its crystals
You swell and you writhe

You open your Buddha gape
You screech at the root of the house

Do not pick up the detonator of the telephone
A flame from the last day will come lashing out of the
    telephone
A dead body will fall out of the telephone

Do not pick up the telephone

Reckless Head

When it comes down to it
Hair is afraid. Words from within are afraid.

They sheer off, like a garment,
Cool, treacherous, no part of you.

Hands the same, feet, and all blood
Till nothing is left. Nothing stays

But what your gaze can carry.
And maybe you vomit even that, like a too-much poison.

Then it is
That the brave hunger of your skull

Supplants you. It stands where you stood
And shouts, with a voice you can't hear,

For what you can't take.

from Prometheus on His Crag

2

Prometheus On His Crag

Relaxes
In the fact that it has happened.

The blue wedge through his breastbone, into the rock,
Unadjusted by vision or prayer – so.

His eyes, brainless police.
His brain, simple as an eye.

Nevertheless, now he exults – like an eagle

In the broadening vastness, the reddening dawn
Of the fact

That cannot be otherwise
And could not have been otherwise,

And never can be otherwise.

And now, for the first time
                              relaxing
                                        helpless

The Titan feels his strength.

3

Prometheus On His Crag

Pestered by birds roosting and defecating,
The chattering static of the wind-honed summit,
The clusterers to heaven, the sun-darkeners –

Shouted a world's end shout.
Then the swallow folded its barbs and fell,
The dove's bubble of fluorescence burst,

Nightingale and cuckoo
Plunged into padded forests where the woodpecker
Eyes bleached insane

Howled laughter into dead holes.

The birds became what birds have ever since been,
Scratching, probing, peering for a lost world –

A world of holy, happy notions shattered
By the shout
That brought Prometheus peace
And woke the vulture.

9

Now I know I never shall

Be let stir.
The man I fashioned and the god I fashioned
Dare not let me stir.

This leakage of cry these face-ripples
Calculated for me – for mountain water
Dammed to powerless stillness.

What secret stays
Stilled under my stillness?
Not even I know.

Only he knows – that bird, that
Filthy-gleeful emissary and
The hieroglyph he makes of my entrails

Is all he tells.

10

Prometheus On His Crag

Began to admire the vulture
It knew what it was doing

It went on doing it
Swallowing not only his liver
But managing also to digest its guilt

And hang itself again just under the sun
Like a heavenly weighing scales
Balancing the gift of life

And the cost of the gift
Without a tremor
As if both were nothing.

14

Prometheus On His Crag

Sees the wind
Whip all things to whip all things
The light whips the water the water whips the light

And men and women are whipped
By invisible tongues
They claw and tear and labour forward

Or cower cornered under the whipping
They whip their animals and their engines
To get them from under the whips

They lift their faces and look all round
For their master and tormentor
When they collapse to curl inwards

They are like cut plants and blind
Already beyond pain or fear
Even the snails are whipped

The swifts too screaming to outstrip the whip
Even as if being were a whipping

Even the earth leaping

Like a great ungainly top

19

Prometheus On His Crag

Shouts and his words
Go off in every direction
Like birds

Like startled birds
They cry the way they fly away
Start up others which follow

For words are the birds of everything –
So soon
Everything is on the wing and gone

So speech starts hopefully to hold
Pieces of the wordy earth together
But pops to space-silence and space-cold

Emptied by words
Scattered and gone.
                  And the mouth shuts
Savagely on a mouthful

Of space-fright which makes the ears ring.

A Violet at Lough Aughresberg

The tide-swell grinds crystal, under cliffs.

Against the opened furnace of the West –
A branch of apple-blossom.

A bullock of sooted bronze
Cools on an emerald
That is crumbling to granite embers.

Milk and blood are frail
In the shivering wind off the sea.

> Only a purple flower – this amulet
> (Once Prospero's) – holds it all, a moment,
> In a rinsed globe of light.

Two Tortoiseshell Butterflies

Mid-May – after May frosts that killed the Camellias,
After May snow. After a winter
Worst in human memory, a freeze
Killing the hundred-year-old Bay Tree,
And the ten-year-old Bay Tree – suddenly
A warm limpness. A blue heaven just veiled
With the sweatings of earth
And with the sweatings-out of winter
Feverish under the piled
Maywear of the lawn.
                              Now two
Tortoiseshell butterflies, finding themselves alive,
She drunk with the earth-sweat, and he

Drunk with her, float in eddies
Over the Daisies' quilt. She prefers Dandelions,
Settling to nod her long spring tongue down
Into the nestling pleats, into the flower's
Thick-folded throat, her wings high-folded.
He settling behind her, among plain glistenings
Of the new grass, edging and twitching
To nearly touch – pulsing and convulsing
Wings wide open to tight-closed to flat open
Quivering to keep her so near, almost reaching
To stroke her abdomen with his antennae –
Then she's up and away, and he startlingly
Swallowlike overtaking, crowding her, heading her
Off any escape. She turns that
To her purpose, and veers down
Onto another Dandelion, attaching
Her weightless yacht to its crest.
Wobbles to stronger hold, to deeper, sweeter
Penetration, her wings tight shut above her,
A sealed book, absorbed in itself.
She ignores him
Where he edges to left and to right, flitting
His wings open, titillating her fur
With his perfumed draughts, spasming his patterns,
His tropical, pheasant appeals of folk-art,
Venturing closer, grass-blade by grass-blade,
Trembling with inhibition, nearly touching –
And again she's away, dithering blackly. He swoops
On an elastic to settle accurately
Under her tail again as she clamps to
This time a Daisy. She's been chosen,
Courtship has claimed her. And he's been conscripted
To what's required
Of the splitting bud, of the talented robin
That performs piercings
Out of the still-bare ash,

The whole air just like him, just breathing
Over the still-turned-inward earth, the first
Caresses of the wedding coming, the earth
Opening its petals, the whole sky
Opening a flower
Of unfathomably-patterned pollen.

Where I Sit Writing My Letter

Suddenly hooligan baby starlings
Rain all round me squealing,
Shouting how it's tremendous and everybody
Has to join in and they're off this minute!

Probably the weird aniseed corpse-odour
Of the hawthorn flower's disturbed them,
As it disturbs me. Now they all rise
Flutter-floating, oddly eddying,

Squalling their dry gargles. Then, mad, they
Hurl off, on a new wrench of excitement,
Leaving me out.
                    I pluck apple-blossom,
Cool, blood-lipped, wet open.

And I'm just quieting thoughts towards my letter
When they all come storming back,
Giddy with hoarse hissings and snarls
And clot the top of an ash sapling –

Sizzling bodies, snaky black necks craning
For a fresh thrill – Where next? Where now? Where? –
    they're off
All rushing after it
Leaving me fevered, and addled.

They can't believe their wings.

Snow-bright clouds boil up.

Tern

for Norman Nicholson

The breaker humps its green glass.
You see the sunrise through it, the wrack dark in it,
And over it – the bird of sickles
Swimming in the wind, with oiled spasm.

That is the tern. A blood-tipped harpoon
Hollow-ground in the roller-dazzle,
Honed in the wind-flash, polished
By his own expertise –

Now finished and in use.
The wings – remote-controlled
By the eyes
In his submarine swift shadow

Feint and tilt in their steel.
Suddenly a triggered magnet
Connects him downward, through a thin shatter,
To a sand-eel. He hoists out, with a twinkling,

Through some other wave-window.
His eye is a gimlet.
Deep in the churned grain of the roller
His brain is a gimlet. He hangs,

A blown tatter, a precarious word
In the mouth of ocean pronouncements.
His meaning has no margin. He shudders
To the tips of his tail-tines.

Momentarily, his lit scrap is a shriek.

The Honey Bee

The Honey Bee
Brilliant as Einstein's idea
Can't be taught a thing.
Like the sun, she's on course forever.

As if nothing else at all existed
Except her flowers.
No mountains, no cows, no beaches, no shops.
Only the rainbow waves of her flowers

A tremor in emptiness

A flying carpet of flowers

                              – a pattern
Coming and going – very loosely woven –
Out of which she works her solutions.

Furry goblin midgets
(The beekeeper's thoughts) clamber stickily
Over the sun's face – gloves of shadow.

But the Honey Bee
Cannot imagine him, in her brilliance,

Though he's a stowaway on her carpet of colour-waves
And drinks her sums.

Sunstruck Foxglove

As you bend to touch
The gypsy girl
Who waits for you in the hedge
Her loose dress falls open.

Midsummer ditch-sickness!

Flushed, freckled with earth-fever,
Swollen lips parted, her eyes closing,
A lolling armful, and so young! Hot

Among the insane spiders.
You glimpse the reptile under-speckle
Of her sunburned breasts
And your head swims. You close your eyes.

Can the foxes talk? Your head throbs.
Remember the bird's tolling echo,
The dripping fern-roots, and the butterfly touches
That woke you.

Remember your mother's
Long, dark dugs.

Her silky body a soft oven
For loaves of pollen.

Eclipse

For half an hour, through a magnifying glass,
I've watched the spiders making love undisturbed,
Ignorant of the voyeur, horribly happy.

First in the lower left-hand corner of the window
I saw an average spider stirring. There
In a midden of carcases, the shambles
Of insects dried in their colours,
A trophy den of uniforms, reds, greens,
Yellow-striped and detached wing-frails, last year's
Leavings, parched a winter, scentless – heads,
Bodices, corsets, leg-shells, a crumble of shards
In a museum of dust and neglect, there
In the crevice, concealed by corpses in their old
    wrappings,

A spider has come to live. She has spun
An untidy nearly invisible
Floss of strands, a few aimless angles
Camouflaged as the grey dirt of the rain-stains
On the glass. I saw her moving. Then a smaller,
Just as ginger, similar all over,
Only smaller. He had suddenly appeared.

Upside down, she was doing a gentle
Sinister dance. All legs clinging
Except for those leading two, which tapped on the web,
Trembling it, I thought, like a fly, to attract
The immobile, upside-down male, near the frame,
Only an inch from her. He moved away,
Turning ready to flee, I guessed. Maybe
Fearful of her intentions and appetites:
Doubting. But her power, focussing,
Making no error after the millions of years
Perfecting this art, turned him round
At a distance of two inches, and hung him
Upside down, head under, belly towards her.
Motionless, except for a faint
And just-detectable throb of his hair-leg tips.
She came closer, upside down, gently,
And enmeshed his forelegs in hers.

So, I imagined, here is the famous murder.
I got closer to watch. Something
Difficult to understand, difficult
To properly observe was going on.
Her two hands seemed swollen, like tiny crab-claws.
Those two nippers she folds up under her nose
To bring things to her pincers, they were moving,
Glistening. He convulsed now and again.
Her abdomen pod twitched -- spasmed slightly
Little mean ecstasies. Was she pulling him to pieces?
Something much more delicate, a much more

Delicate agreement was in process.
Under his abdomen he had a nozzle –
Presumably his lumpy little cock,
Just as ginger as the rest of him, a teat,
An infinitesimal nipple. Probably
Under a microscope it is tooled and designed
Like some micro-device in a space rocket.
To me it looked crude and simple. Far from simple,
Though, were her palps, her boxing-glove nippers –
They were like the mechanical hands
That manipulate radio-active matter
On the other side of safe screen glass.
But hideously dexterous. She reached out one,
I cannot imagine how she saw to do it,
And brought monkey-fingers from under her crab-
nippers
And grasped his nipple cock. As soon as she had it
A bubble of glisteny clear glue
Ballooned up from her nipper, the size of her head,
Then shrank back, and as it shrank back
She wrenched her grip off his cock
As if it had locked there, and doubled her fistful
Of shining wet to her jaw-pincers
And rubbed her mouth and underskin with it,
Six, seven stiff rubs, while her abdomen twitched,
Her tail-tip flirted, and he hung passive.
Then out came her other clutcher, on its elbow,
And grabbed his bud, and the gloy-thick bubble
Swelled above her claws, a red spur flicked
Inside it, and he jerked in his ropes.
Then the bubble shrank and she twisted it off
And brought it back to stuff her face-place
With whatever it was. Very still,
Except for those stealths and those twitchings
They hung upside down, face to face,
Holding forelegs. It was still obscure

Just what was going on. It went on.
Half an hour. Finally she backed off.
He hung like a dead spider, just as he'd hung
All the time she'd dealt with him.
I thought it must be over. So now, I thought,
I see the murder. I could imagine now
If he stirred she'd think he was a fly,
And she'd be feeling ravenous. And so far
She'd shown small excitement about him
With all that concentration on his attachment,
As if he upside down were just the table
Holding the delicacy. She moved off.
Aimlessly awhile she moved round,
Till I realized she was concentrating
On a V of dusty white, a delta
Of floss that seemed just fuzz. Then I could see
How she danced her belly low in the V.
I saw her fitting, with accurate whisker-fine feet,
Blobs of glue to the fibres, and sticking others
To thicken and deepen the V, and knot its juncture.
Then she danced in place, belly down, on this –
Suddenly got up and hung herself
Over the V. Sitting in the cup of the V
Was a tiny blob of new whiteness.
A first egg? Already? Then very carefully
She dabbed at the blob, and worked more woolly fibres
Into the V, to either side of it,
Diminishing it as she dabbed. I could see
I was watching mighty nature
In a purposeful mood, but not what she worked at.
Soon, the little shapeless dot of white
Was a dreg of speck, and she left it. She returned
Towards her male, who hung still in position.
She paused and laboriously cleaned her hands,
Wringing them in her pincers. And suddenly
With a swift, miraculously-accurate snatch

Took something from her mouth, and dumped it
On an outermost cross-strand of web –
A tiny scrap of white – refuse, I thought,
From their lovemaking. So I stopped watching.
Ten minutes later they were at it again.
Now they have vanished. I have scrutinized
The whole rubbish tip of carcases
And the window-frame crannies beneath it.
They are hidden. Is she devouring him now?
Or are there still some days of bliss to come
Before he joins her antiques. They are hidden
Probably together in the fusty dark,
Holding forearms, listening to the rain, rejoicing
As the sun's edge, behind the clouds,
Comes clear of our shadow.

In the Likeness of a Grasshopper

A trap
Waits on the field path.

A wicker contraption, with working parts,
Its spring tensed and set.

So flimsily made, out of grass
(Out of the stems, the joints, the raspy-dry flags).

Baited with a fur-soft caterpillar,
A belly of amorous life, pulsing signals.

Along comes a love-sick, perfume-footed
Music of the wild earth.

The trap, touched by a breath,
Jars into action, its parts blur –

And music cries out.

A sinewy violin
Has caught its violinist.

Cloud-fingered summer, the beautiful trapper,
Picks up the singing cage

And takes out the Song, adds it to the Songs
With which she robes herself, which are her wealth,

Sets her trap again, a yard further on.

New Foal

Yesterday he was nowhere to be found
In the skies or under the skies.

Suddenly he's here – a warm heap
Of ashes and embers, fondled by small draughts.

A star dived from outer space – flared
And burned out in the straw.
Now something is stirring in the smoulder.
We call it a foal.

Still stunned
He has no idea where he is.
His eyes, dew-dusky, explore gloom walls and a glare
    doorspace.
Is this the world?
It puzzles him. It is a great numbness.

He pulls himself together, getting used to the weight of
    things
And to that tall horse nudging him, and to this straw.

He rests
From the first blank shock of light, the empty daze
Of the questions –
What has happened? What am I?

His ears keep on asking, gingerly.

But his legs are impatient,
Recovering from so long being nothing
They are restless with ideas, they start to try a few out,

Angling this way and that,
Feeling for leverage, learning fast –

And suddenly he's up

And stretching – a giant hand
Strokes him from nose to heel
Perfecting his outline, as he tightens
The knot of himself.
                                Now he comes teetering
Over the weird earth. His nose
Downy and magnetic, draws him, incredulous,
Towards his mother. And the world is warm
And careful and gentle. Touch by touch
Everything fits him together.

Soon he'll be almost a horse.
He wants only to be Horse,
Pretending each day more and more Horse
Till he's perfect Horse. Then unearthly Horse
Will surge through him, weightless, a spinning of flame
Under sudden gusts,

It will coil his eyeball and his heel
In a single terror – like the awe
Between lightning and thunderclap.

And curve his neck, like a sea-monster emerging
Among foam,

And fling the new moons through his stormy banner,
And the full moons and the dark moons.

The Hen

The Hen
Worships the dust. She finds God everywhere.
Everywhere she finds his jewels.

And she does not care
What the cabbage thinks.

She has forgotten flight
Because she has interpreted happily
Her recurrent dream
Of clashing cleavers, of hot ovens,
And of the little pen-knife blade
Splitting her palate.
She flaps her wings, like shallow egg-baskets,
To show her contempt
For those who live on escape
And a future of empty sky.

She rakes, with noble, tireless foot,
The treasury of the dirt,
And clucks with the mechanical alarm clock
She chose instead of song
When the Creator
Separated the Workers and the Singers.

With her eye on reward
She tilts her head religiously
At the most practical angle
Which reveals to her
That the fox is a country superstition,
That her eggs have made man her slave
And that the heavens, for all their threatening,
Have not yet fallen.

And she is stern. Her eye is fierce – blood
(That weakness) is punished instantly.
She is a hard bronze of uprightness.
And indulges herself in nothing
Except to swoon a little, a delicious slight swoon,
One eye closed, just before sleep,
Conjuring the odour of tarragon.

The Hare

I

That Elf
Riding his awkward pair of haunchy legs

That weird long-eared Elf
Wobbling down the highway

Don't overtake him, don't try to drive past him,
He's scatty, he's all over the road,
He can't keep his steering, in his ramshackle go-cart,
His big loose wheels, buckled and rusty,
Nearly wobbling off

And all the screws in his head wobbling and loose

And his eyes wobbling

II

The Hare is a very fragile thing.
The life in the hare is a glassy goblet, and her yellow-
    fringed frost-flake belly says: Fragile.

The hare's bones are light glass. And the hare's face –

Who lifted her face to the Lord?
Her new-budded nostrils and lips,
For the daintiest pencillings, the last eyelash touches

Delicate as the down of a moth,
And the breath of awe
Which fixed the mad beauty-light
In her look
As if her retina
Were a moon perpetually at full.

Who is it, at midnight on the A30,
The Druid soul,

The night-streaker, the sudden lumpy goblin
That thumps your car under the belly
Then cries with human pain
And becomes a human baby on the road
That you dare hardly pick up?

Or leaps, like a long bat with little headlights,
Straight out of darkness
Into the driver's nerves
With a jangle of cries
As if the car had crashed into a flying harp

So that the driver's nerves flail and cry
Like a burst harp.

III

Uneasy she nears
As if she were being lured, but fearful,
Nearer.
Like a large egg toppling itself – mysterious!

Then she'll stretch, tall, on her hind feet,
And lean on the air,
Taut – like a stilled yacht waiting on the air –

And what does the hunter see? A fairy woman?
A dream beast?
A kangaroo of the March corn?

The loveliest face listening,
Her black-tipped ears hearing the bud of the blackthorn
Opening its lips,
Her black-tipped hairs hearing tomorrow's weather
Combing the mare's tails,
Her snow-fluff belly feeling for the first breath,
Her orange nape, foxy with its dreams of the fox –

Witch-maiden
Heavy with trembling blood – astounding
How much blood there is in her body!
She is a moony pond of quaking blood

Twitched with spells, her gold-ringed eye spellbound –

Carrying herself so gently, balancing
Herself with the gentlest touches
As if her eyes brimmed –

IV

I've seen her,
A lank, lean hare, with her long thin feet
And her long, hollow thighs,
And her ears like ribbons
Careering by moonlight
In her Flamenco, her heels flinging the dust
On the drum of the hill.

And I've seen him, hobbling stiffly
God of Leapers
Surprised by dawn, earth-bound, and stained
With drying mud,
Painfully rocking over the furrows

With his Leaping-Legs, his Power-Thighs
Much too powerful for ordinary walking,
So powerful
They seem almost a burden, almost a problem,
Nearly an aching difficulty for him
When he tries to loiter or pause,
Nearly a heaving pain to lift and move
Like turning a cold car-engine with a bent crank handle –

Till a shock, a terror, with a bang
Grabs at her ears. An oven door
Bangs open, both barrels, and a barking

Bursts out of onions –
                    and she leaps
And her heels
Hard as angle-iron kick salt and pepper
Into the lurcher's eyes –
                    and kick and kick
The spinning, turnip world
Into the lurcher's gullet –
                    as she slips
Between thin hawthorn and thinner bramble
Into tomorrow.

The River

Fallen from heaven, lies across
The lap of his mother, broken by world.

But water will go on
Issuing from heaven

In dumbness uttering spirit brightness
Through its broken mouth.

Scattered in a million pieces and buried
Its dry tombs will split, at a sign in the sky,

At a rending of veils.
It will rise, in a time after times,

After swallowing death and the pit
It will return stainless

For the delivery of this world.
So the river is a god

Knee-deep among reeds, watching men,
Or hung by the heels down the door of a dam

It is a god, and inviolable.
Immortal. And will wash itself of all deaths.

Milesian Encounter on the Sligachan

for Hilary and Simon

'Up in the pools,' they'd said, and 'Two miles upstream.'

Something sinister about bogland rivers.

And a shock –

after the two miles of tumblequag, of Ice-Age hairi-
ness, crusty, quaking cadaver and me lurching over it
in elation like a daddy-long-legs –

after crooked little clatterbrook and again clatterbrook
(a hurry of shallow grey light so distilled it looked like
acid) –

and after the wobbly levels of a razor-edged, blood-
smeared grass, the flood-sucked swabs of bog-cotton,
the dusty calico rip-up of snipe –

under those petrified scapulae, vertebrae, horn-
skulls the Cuillins (asylum of eagles) that were blue-
silvered like wrinkled baking foil in the blue noon that
day, and tremulous –

early August, in a hot lateness (only three hours
before my boat), a glimpse of my watch and suddenly

up to my hip in a suck-hole then on again teetering
over the broken-necked heath-bobs a good half-hour
and me melting in my combined fuel of toil and
clobber suddenly

The shock.
The sheer cavern of current piling silence
Under my feet.

So lonely-drowning deep, so drowned-hair silent
So clear
Cleansing the body cavity of the underbog.

Such a brilliant cut-glass interior
Sliding under me

And I felt a little bit giddy
Ghostly
As I fished the long pool-tail
Peering into that superabundance of spirit.

And now where were they, my fellow aliens from
    prehistory?
Those peculiar eyes
So like mine, but fixed at zero,
Pressing in from outer darkness
Eyes of aimed sperm and of egg on their errand,
Looking for immortality
In the lap of a broken volcano, in the furrow of a lost
    glacier,
Those shuttles of love-shadow?

Only humbler beings waved at me –
Weeds grazing the bottom, idling their tails.

Till the last pool –
A broad, coiling whorl, a deep ear
Of pondering amber,
Greenish and precious like a preservative,
With a ram's skull sunk there – magnified, a Medusa,
Funereal, phosphorescent, a lamp
Ten feet under the whisky.

I heard this pool whisper a warning.

I tickled its leading edges with temptation.
I stroked its throat with a whisker.
I licked the moulded hollows
Of its collarbones
Where the depth, now underbank opposite,
Pulsed up from contained excitements –

Eerie how you know when it's coming –
So I felt it now, my blood
Prickling and thickening, altering
With an ushering-in of chills, a weird onset
As if mountains were pushing mountains higher
Behind me, to crowd over my shoulder –

Then the pool lifted a travelling bulge
And grabbed the tip of my heart-nerve, and crashed,

Trying to wrench it from me, and again
Lifted a flash of arm for leverage
And it was a Gruagach of the Sligachan!
Some Boggart up from a crack in the granite!
A Glaistig out of the skull!
                              – what was it gave me
Such a supernatural, beautiful fright

And let go, and sank disembodied
Into the eye-pupil darkness?

Only a little salmon.
                              Salmo salar
The loveliest, left-behind, most-longed-for ogress
Of the Palaeolithic
Watched me through her time-warped judas-hole
In the ruinous castle of Skye

As I faded from the light of reality.

Low Water

                              This evening
The river is a beautiful idle woman.

The day's August burn-out has distilled
A heady sundowner.
She lies back, bored and tipsy.

She lolls on her deep couch. And a long thigh
Lifts from the flash of her silks.

Adoring trees, kneeling, ogreish eunuchs
Comb out her spread hair, massage her fingers.

She stretches – and an ecstasy tightens
Over her skin, and deep in her gold body

Thrills spasm and dissolve. She drowses.

Her half-dreams lift out of her, light-minded
Love-pact suicides. Copulation and death.

She stirs her love-potion – ooze of balsam
Thickened with fish-mucus and algae.

You stand under leaves, your feet in shallows.
She eyes you steadily from the beginning of the world.

Japanese River Tales

I

Tonight
From the swaddled village, down the padded lane
Snow is hurrying
To the tryst, is touching
At her hair, at her raiment
Glint-slippered
Over the stubble,
                    naked under
Her light robe, jewels
In her hair, in her ears, at her bare throat
Dark eye-flash
                    twigs and brambles
Catch at her
            as she lifts

The raggy curtains
Of the river's hovel, and plunges
Into his grasping bed.

II

The lithe river rejoices all morning
In his juicy bride – the snow princess
Who peeped from clouds, and chose him,
                and descended.

The tale goes on
With glittery laughter of immortals
Shaking the alders –
In the end a drowsy after-bliss
Blue-hazes the long valley. High gulls
Look down on the flash
And languor of suppled shoulders
Bedded in her ermine.
                Night
Lifts off the illusion. Lifts
The beauty from her skull. The sockets, in fact,
Are root-arches – empty
To ashes of stars. Her kiss
Grips through the full throat and locks
On the dislodged vertebrae.
                        Her talons
Lengthened by moonlight, numb open
The long belly of blood.
                        And the river
Is a gutter of death,
A spill of glitters
                dangling from her grasp
As she flies
Through the shatter of space and
Out of being.

Ophelia

Where the pool unfurls its undercloud –
There she goes.

And through and through
The kneading tumble and the water-hammer.

If a trout leaps into air, it is not for a breather.
It has to drop back immediately

Into this peculiar engine
That made it, and keeps it going,

And that works it to death –
                    there she goes

Darkfish, finger to her lips,
Staringly into the afterworld.

Strangers

Dawn. The river thins.
The combed-out coiffure at the pool-tail
Brightens thinly.
The slung pool's long hammock still flat out.

The sea-trout, a salt flotilla, at anchor,
Substanceless, flame-shadowed,
Hang in a near emptiness of sunlight.

There they actually are, under homebody oaks,
Close to teddybear sheep, near purple loose-strife –

Space-helms bowed in preoccupation,
Only a slight riffling of their tail-ailerons
Corrective of drift,
Gills easing.

And the pool's toiled rampart roots,
The cavorting of new heifers, water-skeeters
On their abacus, even the slow claim
Of the buzzard's hand
Merely decorate a heaven
Where the sea-trout, fixed and pouring,
Lean in the speed of light.
                    And make nothing
Of the strafed hogweed sentry skeletons,
Nothing of the sun, so openly aiming down.

Thistle-floss bowls over them. First, lost leaves
Feel over them with blind shadows.

The sea-trout, upstaring, in trance,
Absorb everything and forget it
Into a blank of bliss.

And this is the real samadhi – worldless, levitated.

Till, bulging, a man-shape
Wobbles their firmament.
                    Now see the holy ones
Shrink their auras, slim, sink, focus, prepare
To scram like trout.

The Gulkana

Jumbled iceberg hills, away to the North –
And a long wreath of fire-haze.

The Gulkana, where it meets the Copper,
Swung, jade, out of the black spruce forest,
And disappeared into it.

Strange word, Gulkana. What does it mean?
A pre-Columbian glyph.
A pale blue thread – scrawled with a child's hand

Across our map. A Lazarus of water
Returning from seventy below.
                                We stumbled,
Not properly awake
In a weird light – a bombardment
Of purplish emptiness –
Among phrases that lumped out backwards. Among
    rocks
That kept startling me – too rock-like,
Hypnagogic rocks –
                        A scrapyard of boxy shacks
And supermarket refuse, dogs, wrecked pick-ups,
The Indian village where we bought our pass
Was comatose – on the stagnation toxins
Of a cultural vasectomy. They were relapsing
To Cloud-like-a-boulder, Mica, Bear, Magpie.

We hobbled along a tightrope shore of pebbles
Under a trickling bluff
That bounced the odd pebble onto us, eerily.
(The whole land was in perpetual, seismic tremor.)
Gulkana –
Biblical, a deranging cry
From the wilderness – burst past us.
A stone voice that dragged at us.
I found myself clinging
To the lifted skyline fringe of rag spruce
And the subsidence under my bootsoles
With balancing glances – nearly a fear,
Something I kept trying to deny

With deliberate steps. But it came with me
As if it swayed on my pack –
A nape-of-the-neck unease. We'd sploshed far enough
Through the spongy sinks of the permafrost
For this river's
Miraculous fossils – creatures that each midsummer

Resurrected through it, in a blood-rich flesh.
Pilgrims for a fish!
Prospectors for the lode in a fish's eye!

In that mercury light, that ultra-violet,
My illusion developed. I felt hunted.
I tested my fear. It seemed to live in my neck –
A craven, bird-headed alertness.
And in my eye
That felt blind somehow to what I stared at
As if it stared at me. And in my ear –
So wary for the air-stir in the spruce-tips
My ear-drum almost ached. I explained it
To my quietly arguing, lucid panic
As my fear of one inside me,
A bodiless twin, some doppelgänger
Disinherited other, unliving,
Ever-living, a larva from prehistory,
Whose journey this was, who now exulted
Recognizing his home,
And whose gaze I could feel as he watched me
Fiddling with my gear – the interloper,
The fool he had always hated. We pitched our tent

And for three days
Our tackle scratched the windows of the express torrent.

We seemed underpowered. Whatever we hooked
Bent in air, a small porpoise,
Then went straight downriver under the weight
And joined the glacial landslide of the Copper
Which was the colour of cement.

Even when we got one ashore
It was too big to eat.

But there was the eye!
                    · I peered into that lens

Seeking what I had come for. (What had I come for?
The camera-flash? The burned-out, ogling bulb?)
What I saw was small, crazed, snake-like.
It made me think of a dwarf, shrunken sun
And of the black, refrigerating pressures
Under the Bering Sea.

We relaunched their mulberry-dark torsos,
Those gulping, sooted mouths, the glassy visors –

Arks of an undelivered covenant,
Egg-sacs of their own Eden,
Seraphs of heavy ore

They surged away, magnetized,
Into the furnace boom of the Gulkana.

Bliss had fixed their eyes
Like an anaesthetic. They were possessed
By that voice in the river
And its accompaniment –
The flutes, the drumming. And they rose and sank
Like voices, themselves like singers
In its volume. We watched them, deepening away.
They looked like what they were, somnambulists,
Drugged, ritual victims, melting away
Towards a sacrament –
                              a consummation
That could only be death.
Which it would be, within some numbered days,
On some stony platform of water,
In a spillway, where a man could hardly stand –
Aboriginal Americans,
High among rains, in an opening of the hills,
They will begin to circle,
Shedding their ornaments,
In shufflings and shudders, male by female,
Begin to dance their deaths –

The current hosing over their brows and shoulders,
Bellies riven open and shaken empty
Into a gutter of pebbles
In the orgy of eggs and sperm,
The dance orgy of being reborn
From which masks and regalia drift empty,
Torn off – at last their very bodies,
In the numbed, languorous frenzy, as obstacles,
Ripped away –
                        ecstasy dissolving
In the mercy of water, at the star of the source,
Devoured by revelation,
Every molecule drained, and counted, and healed
Into the amethyst of emptiness –

I came back to myself. A spectre of fragments
Lifted my quivering coffee, in the aircraft,
And sipped at it.
I imagined the whole 747
As if a small boy held it
Making its noise. A spectre,
Escaping the film's flicker, peered from the porthole
Under the sun's cobalt core-darkness
Down at Greenland's corpse
Tight-sheeted with snow-glare.
                        Word by word
The voice of the river moved in me.
It was like lovesickness.
A numbness, a secret bleeding.
Waking in my body.
                        Telling of the King
Salmon's eye.
                        Of the blood-mote mosquito.

And the stilt-legged, subarctic, one-rose rose
With its mock-aperture

Tilting towards us
In our tent-doorway, its needle tremor.

And the old Indian Headman, in his tatty jeans and
    socks, who smiled
Adjusting to our incomprehension – his face
A whole bat, that glistened and stirred.

Go Fishing

Join water, wade in underbeing
Let brain mist into moist earth
Ghost loosen away downstream
Gulp river and gravity

Lose words
Cease
Be assumed into glistenings of lymph
As if creation were a wound
As if this flow were all plasm healing

Be supplanted by mud and leaves and pebbles
By sudden rainbow monster-structures
That materialize in suspension gulping
And dematerialize under pressure of the eye

Be cleft by the sliding prow
Displaced by the hull of light and shadow

Dissolved in earth-wave, the soft sun-shock,
Dismembered in sun-melt

Become translucent – one untangling drift
Of water-mesh, and a weight of earth-taste light
Mangled by wing-shadows
Everything circling and flowing and hover-still

Crawl out over roots, new and nameless
Search for face, harden into limbs

Let the world come back, like a white hospital
Busy with urgency words

Try to speak and nearly succeed
Heal into time and other people

Salmon Eggs

The salmon were just down there –
Shivering together, touching at each other,
Shedding themselves for each other –

Now beneath flood-murmur
They peel away deathwards.

                   January haze,
With a veined yolk of sun. In bone-damp cold
I lean and watch the water, listening to water
Till my eyes forget me

And the piled flow supplants me, the mud-blooms

All this ponderous light of everlasting
Collapsing away under its own weight

Mastodon ephemera

Mud-curdling, bull-dozing, hem-twinkling
Caesarean of Heaven and Earth, unfelt

With exhumations and delirious advents --

                Catkins
Wriggle at their mother's abundance. The spider clings to
   his craft.

Something else is going on in the river

More vital than death – death here seems a superficiality
Of small scaly limbs, parasitical. More grave than life
Whose reflex jaws and famished crystals
Seem incidental
To this telling – these tidings of plasm –
The melt of mouthing silence, the charge of light
Dumb with immensity.

                            The river goes on
Sliding through its place, undergoing itself
In its wheel.

                            I make out the sunk foundations
Of dislocated crypts, a bedrock
Time-hewn, time-riven altar. And this is the liturgy
Of Earth's advent – harrowing, crowned – a travail
Of raptures and rendings. Perpetual mass
Of the waters
Wells from the cleft.
                            This is the swollen vent
Of the nameless
Teeming inside atoms – and inside the haze
And inside the sun and inside the earth.

It is the font, brimming with touch and whisper,
Swaddling the egg.
                    Only birth matters
Say the river's whorls.
                            And the river
Silences everything in a leaf-mouldering hush
Where sun rolls bare, and earth rolls,

And mind condenses on old haws.

A Cormorant

Here before me, snake-head
My waders weigh seven pounds.

My Barbour jacket, mainly necessary
For its pockets, is proof

Against the sky at my back. My bag
Sags with lures and hunter's medicine enough

For a year in the Pleistocene.
My hat, of use only

If this May relapses to March,
Embarrasses me, and my net, long as myself,

Optimistic, awkward, infatuated
With every twig-snag and fence-barb

Will slowly ruin the day. I paddle
Precariously on slimed shale,

And infiltrate twenty yards
Of gluey and magnetized spider-gleam

Into the elbowing dense jostle-traffic
Of the river's tunnel, and pray

With futuristic, archaic under-breath
So that some fish, telepathically overpowered,

Will attach its incomprehension
To the bauble I offer to space in general.

The cormorant eyes me, beak uptilted,
Body snake-low – sea-serpentish.

He's thinking: 'Will that stump
Stay a stump just while I dive?' He dives.

He sheds everything from his tail end
Except fish-action, becomes fish,

Disappears from bird,
Dissolving himself

Into fish, so dissolving fish naturally
Into himself. Re-emerges, gorged,

Himself as he was, and escapes me.
Leaves me high and dry in my space-armour,

A deep-sea diver in two inches of water.

An Eel

I

The strange part is his head. Her head. The strangely
   ripened
Domes over the brain, swollen nacelles
For some large containment. Lobed glands
Of some large awareness. Eerie the eel's head.
This full, plum-sleeked fruit of evolution.
Beneath it, her snout's a squashed slipper-face,
The mouth grin-long and perfunctory,
Undershot predatory. And the iris, dirty gold
Distilled only enough to be different
From the olive lode of her body,
The grained and woven blacks. And ringed larger
With a vaguer vision, an earlier eye
Behind her eye, paler, blinder,
Inward. Her buffalo hump
Begins the amazement of her progress.
Her mid-shoulder pectoral fin – concession
To fish-life – secretes itself
Flush with her concealing suit: under it

The skin's a pale exposure of deepest eel
As her belly is, a dulled pearl.
Strangest, the thumb-print skin, the rubberized weave
Of her insulation. Her whole body
Damascened with identity. This is she
Suspends the Sargasso
In her inmost hope. Her life is a cell
Sealed from event, her patience
Global and furthered with love
By the bending stars as if she
Were earth's sole initiate. Alone
In her millions, the moon's pilgrim,
The nun of water.

II

Where does the river come from?
And the eel, the night-mind of water –
The river within the river and opposite –
The night-nerve of water?

Not from the earth's remembering mire
Not from the air's whim
Not from the brimming sun. Where from?

From the bottom of the nothing pool
Sargasso of God
Out of the empty spiral of stars

A glimmering person

Performance

Just before the curtain falls in the river
The Damselfly, with offstage, inaudible shriek
Reappears, weightless.

Hover-poised, in her snake-skin leotards,
Her violet-dark elegance.

Eyelash-delicate, a dracula beauty,
In her acetylene jewels.

Her mascara smudged, her veils shimmer-fresh –

Late August. Some sycamore leaves
Already in their museum, eaten to lace.
Robin song bronze-touching the stillness
Over posthumous nettles. The swifts, as one,
Whipcracked, gone. Blackberries.
                          And now, lightly,
Adder-shock of this dainty assassin
Still in mid-passion –
                  still in her miracle play:
Masked, archaic, mute, insect mystery
Out of the sun's crypt.
                  Everything is forgiven
Such a metamorphosis in love!
Phaedra Titania
Dragon of crazed enamels!
Tragedienne of the ultra-violet,
So sulphurous and so frail,

Stepping so magnetically to her doom!

Lifted out of the river with tweezers
Dripping the sun's incandescence –
                          suddenly she
Switches her scene elsewhere.

        (Find him later, halfway up a nettle,
        A touch-crumple petal of web and dew –

        Midget puppet-clown, tranced on his strings,
        In the nightfall pall of balsam.)

Night Arrival of Sea-Trout

Honeysuckle hanging her fangs.
Foxglove rearing her open belly.
Dogrose touching the membrane.

Through the dew's mist, the oak's mass
Comes plunging, tossing dark antlers.

Then a shattering
Of the river's hole, where something leaps out –

An upside-down, buried heaven
Snarls, moon-mouthed, and shivers.

Summer dripping stars, biting at the nape.
Lobworms coupling in saliva.
Earth singing under her breath.

And out in the hard corn a horned god
Running and leaping
With a bat in his drum.

October Salmon

He's lying in poor water, a yard or so depth of poor
    safety,
Maybe only two feet under the no-protection of an
    outleaning small oak,
Half under a tangle of brambles.

After his two thousand miles, he rests,
Breathing in that lap of easy current
In his graveyard pool.

About six pounds weight,
Four years old at most, and hardly a winter at sea –
But already a veteran,
Already a death-patched hero. So quickly it's over!

So briefly he roamed the gallery of marvels!
Such sweet months, so richly embroidered into earth's
    beauty-dress,
Her life-robe –
Now worn out with her tirelessness, her insatiable quest,
Hangs in the flow, a frayed scarf –

An autumnal pod of his flower,
The mere hull of his prime, shrunk at shoulder and
    flank,

With the sea-going Aurora Borealis
Of his April power –
The primrose and violet of that first upfling in the
    estuary –
Ripened to muddy dregs,
The river reclaiming his sea-metals.

In the October light
He hangs there, patched with leper-cloths.

Death has already dressed him
In her clownish regimentals, her badges and decorations,
Mapping the completion of his service,
His face a ghoul-mask, a dinosaur of senility, and his
    whole body
A fungoid anemone of canker –

Can the caress of water ease him?
The flow will not let up for a minute.

What a change! from that covenant of polar light
To this shroud in a gutter!
What a death-in-life – to be his own spectre!
His living body become death's puppet,
Dolled by death in her crude paints and drapes
He haunts his own staring vigil
And suffers the subjection, and the dumbness,
And the humiliation of the role!

And that is how it is,
That is what is going on there, under the scrubby oak
    tree, hour after hour,
That is what the splendour of the sea has come down to,
And the eye of ravenous joy – king of infinite liberty
In the flashing expanse, the bloom of sea-life,

On the surge-ride of energy, weightless,
Body simply the armature of energy
In that earliest sea-freedom, the savage amazement of
    life,
The salt mouthful of actual existence
With strength like light –

Yet this was always with him. This was inscribed in his
    egg.
This chamber of horrors is also home.
He was probably hatched in this very pool.

And this was the only mother he ever had, this uneasy
    channel of minnows
Under the mill-wall, with bicycle wheels, car tyres,
    bottles
And sunk sheets of corrugated iron.
People walking their dogs trail their evening shadows
    across him.
If boys see him they will try to kill him.

All this, too, is stitched into the torn richness,
The epic poise
That holds him so steady in his wounds, so loyal to his
    doom, so patient
In the machinery of heaven.

That Morning

We came where the salmon were so many
So steady, so spaced, so far-aimed
On their inner map, England could add

Only the sooty twilight of South Yorkshire
Hung with the drumming drift of Lancasters
Till the world had seemed capsizing slowly.

Solemn to stand there in the pollen light
Waist-deep in wild salmon swaying massed
As from the hand of God. There the body

Separated, golden and imperishable,
From its doubting thought – a spirit-beacon
Lit by the power of the salmon

That came on, came on, and kept on coming
As if we flew slowly, their formations
Lifting us toward some dazzle of blessing

One wrong thought might darken. As if the fallen
World and salmon were over. As if these
Were the imperishable fish

That had let the world pass away –

There, in a mauve light of drifted lupins,
They hung in the cupped hands of mountains

Made of tingling atoms. It had happened.
Then for a sign that we were where we were
Two gold bears came down and swam like men

Beside us. And dived like children.
And stood in deep water as on a throne
Eating pierced salmon off their talons.

So we found the end of our journey.

So we stood, alive in the river of light
Among the creatures of light, creatures of light.

Astrological Conundrums

I THE FOOL'S EVIL DREAM

I was just walking about.
Trees here, trees there, ferny accompaniment.
Rocks sticking through their moss jerseys.
A twilight like smoked spectacles, depressive.

I saw a glowing beast – a tigress.
Only different with flower-smells, wet-root smells,
Fish-still-alive-from-their-weed-river smells
And eyes that hurt me with beauty.

She wanted to play so we gambolled.
She promised to show me her cave
Which was the escape route from death
And which came out into a timeless land.

To find this cave, she said, we lie down
And you hold me, so, and we fly.
So it was I came to be folded
In the fur of a tiger. And as we travelled

She told me of a very holy man
Who fed himself to a tigress
Because hunger had dried up her milk
And as he filled her belly he became

The never-dying god who gives everything
Which he had always wanted to be.
As I heard her story I dissolved
In the internal powers of tiger

And passed through a dim land
Swinging under her backbone. Till I heard
A sudden cry of fear, an infant's cry –
Close, as if my own ear had cried it.

I sat up
Wet and alone
Among starry rocks.

A bright spirit went away weeping.

II NEARLY AWAKE

The bulls swing their headweights,
Eyes bulging storms and moon-terrors.
Their cleft roots creak all round you
Where you lie, face-bedded, vegetable.

A frozen stone – the stone of your headbone.
The Universe flies dark.
The bulls bulk darker, as their starred nostrils
Blow and ponder your spine.

You lie, helpless as grass. Your prayer,
Petrified into the earth's globe,
Supports you, a crest of fear
On its unstirring.

The wild bulls of your mother have found you.
Huge nudgings of blood, sperm, saliva
Rasp you alive, towel you awake with tongues.
Now they start gnawing the small of your back.

The cry you dare not cry in these moments
Will last you a lifetime.

III TELL

This was my dream. Suddenly my old steel bow
Sprang into my hand and my whole body

Leaned into the bend a harp frame
So perfectly strung it seemed weightless.

I saw the Raven sitting alone
On the crest of the globe. I could see
The Raven's eye agleam in the sky river
Like an emblem on a flowing banner.

I saw the Raven's eye watching me
Through the slitted fabric of the skyflow.
I bent the bow's full weight against the star
In that eye until I could see nothing

But that star. Then as I sank my aim
Deeper into the star that had grown
To fill the Universe I heard a whisper:
'Be careful. I'm here. Don't forget me.'

With all my might – I hesitated.

Dust As We Are

My post-war father was so silent
He seemed to be listening. I eavesdropped
On the hot line. His lonely sittings
Mangled me, in secret – like TV
Watched too long, my nerves lasered.
Then, an after image of the incessant
Mowing passage of machine-gun effects,
What it filled a trench with. And his laugh
(How had that survived – so nearly intact?)
Twitched the curtain never quite deftly enough
Over the hospital wards
Crowded with his (photographed) shock-eyed pals.

I had to use up a lot of spirit
Getting over it. I was helping him.

I was his supplementary convalescent.
He took up his pre-war *joie de vivre*.
But his displays of muscular definition
Were a bleached montage – lit landscapes:
Swampquakes of the slime of puddled soldiers
Where bones and bits of equipment
Showered from every shell-burst.
                              Naked men
Slithered staring where their mothers and sisters
Would never have to meet their eyes, or see
Exactly how they sprawled and were trodden.

So he had been salvaged and washed.
His muscles very white – marble white.
He had been heavily killed. But we had revived him.
Now he taught us a silence like prayer.
There he sat, killed but alive – so long
As we were very careful. I divined,
With a comb,
Under his wavy, golden hair, as I combed it,
The fragility of skull. And I filled
With his knowledge.
                      After mother's milk
This was the soul's food. A soap-smell spectre
Of the massacre of innocents. So the soul grew.
A strange thing, with rickets – a hyena.
No singing – that kind of laughter.

Telegraph Wires

Take telegraph wires, a lonely moor,
And fit them together. The thing comes alive in your ear.

Towns whisper to towns over the heather.
But the wires cannot hide from the weather.

So oddly, so daintily made
It is picked up and played.

Such unearthly airs
The ear hears, and withers!

In the revolving ballroom of space,
Bowed over the moor, a bright face

Draws out of telegraph wires the tones
That empty human bones.

Sacrifice

Born at the bottom of the heap. And as he grew upwards
The welts of his brow deepened, fold upon fold.
Like the Tragic Mask.
Cary Grant was his living double.

They said: When he was little he'd drop
And kick and writhe, and kick and cry:
'I'll break my leg! I'll break my leg!'
Till he'd ground his occiput bald.

While the brothers built cords, moleskins, khakis
Into dynastic, sweated ziggurats,
His fateful forehead sank
Away among Westerns, the ruts of the Oregon Trail.

Screwdriver, drill, chisel, saw, hammer
Were less than no use.
A glass-fronted cabinet was his showpiece.
His wife had locked him in there with the china.

His laugh jars at my ear. That laugh
Was an elastic vault into freedom.
Sound as a golfball.
He'd belt it into the blue.

He never drank in a bar. When he stood
Before he'd stepped she'd plumped the cushions beneath
   him.
So perfectly kept.
Sundays they drove here and there in the car.

An armchair Samson. Baffled and shorn
His dream bulged into forearms
That performed their puppet-play of muscles
To make a nephew stare. He and I

Lammed our holly billets across Banksfields –
A five-inch propeller climbing the skylines
For two, three seconds – to the drop. And the paced-out
   length
Of his leash! The limit of human strength!

Suddenly he up and challenged
His brothers for a third of the partnership.
The duumvirate of wives turned down their thumbs.
Brotherly concern – Rain from Rochdale!

Snow from Halifax! Stars over valley walls!
His fireside escape
Simple as leaping astride a bare-back pinto
Was a kick at the ceiling, and that laugh.

He toiled in his attic after midnight
Mass-producing toy ducks
On wooden wheels, that went with clicks.
Flight! Flight!

The brothers closed their eyes. They quivered their jowls:
British Columbia's the place for a chap like thee!
The lands of the future! Look at Australia –
Crying out for timber buildings! Get out there!

On the canal bridge bend, at Hawkscluffe,
A barrel bounced off a lorry.

His motorbike hit the wall.
'I just flew straight up – and when I dropped

I missed the canal! I actually missed the canal!
I nearly broke the bank! For once
I landed smack on my feet!
My shoelaces burst from top to bottom!'

His laugh thumped my body.
When he tripped
The chair from beneath him, in his attic,
Midsummer dusk, his sister, forty miles off,

Cried out at the hammer blow on her nape.
And his daughter
Who'd climbed up to singsong: 'Supper, Daddy'
Fell back down the stairs to the bottom.

For the Duration

I felt a strange fear when the war-talk,
Like a creeping barrage, approached you.
Jig and jag I'd fitted much of it together.
Our treasure, your D.C.M. – again and again
Carrying in the wounded
Collapsing with exhaustion. And as you collapsed
A shell-burst
Just in front of you lifting you upright
For the last somnambulist yards
Before you fell under your load into the trench.
The shell, some other time, that buried itself
Between your feet as you walked
And thoughtfully failed to go off.
The shrapnel hole, over your heart – how it spun you.
The blue scar of the bullet at your ankle
From a traversing machine-gun that tripped you

As you cleared the parapet. Meanwhile
The horrors were doled out, everybody
Had his appalling tale.
But what alarmed me most
Was your silence. Your refusal to tell.
I had to hear from others
What you survived and what you did.

Maybe you didn't want to frighten me.
Now it's too late.
Now I'd ask you shamelessly.
But then I felt ashamed.
What was my shame? Why couldn't I have borne
To hear you telling what you underwent?
Why was your war so much more unbearable
Than anybody else's? As if nobody else
Knew how to remember. After some uncle's
Virtuoso tale of survival
That made me marvel and laugh –
I looked at your face, your cigarette
Like a dial-finger. And my mind
Stopped with numbness.

Your day-silence was the coma
Out of which your night-dreams rose shouting.
I could hear you from my bedroom –
The whole hopelessness still going on,
No man's land still crying and burning
Inside our house, and you climbing again
Out of the trench, and wading back into the glare

As if you might still not manage to reach us
And carry us to safety.

Walt

Going up for the assault that morning
They passed the enclosure of prisoners.
'A big German stood at the wire,' he said,
'A big German, and he caught my eye.
And he cursed me. I felt his eye curse me.'

Halfway up the field, the bullet
Hit him in the groin. He rolled
Into a shell-hole. The sun rose and burned.
A sniper clipped his forehead. He wormed
Deeper down. Bullet after bullet
Dug at the crater rim, searching for him.
Another clipped him. Then the sniper stopped.

All that day he lay. He went walks
Along the Heights Road, from Peckett to Midgley,
Down to Mytholmroyd (past Ewood
Of his ancestors, past the high-perched factory
Of his future life). Up the canal bank,
Up Redacre, along and down into Hebden,
Then up into Crimsworth Dene, to their old campground
In the happy valley.
And up over Shackleton Hill, to Widdop,
Back past Greenwood Lea, above Hardcastles,
To Heptonstall – all day
He walked about the valley, as he lay
Under High Wood in the shell-hole.

I knew the knot of scar on his temple.

We stood in the young March corn
Of a perfect field. His fortune made.
His life's hope over. Me beside him
Just the age he'd been when that German

Took aim with his eye and hit him so hard
It brought him and his wife down together,
With all his children one after the other.

A misty rain prickled and hazed.
'Here,' he hazarded. 'Somewhere just about here.
This is where he stopped me. I got this far.'

He frowned uphill towards the skyline tree-fringe
As through binoculars
Towards all that was left.

II THE ATLANTIC

Night after night he'd sat there,
Eighty-four, still telling the tale.
With his huge thirst for anaesthetics.
'Time I were dead,' I'd heard. 'I want to die.'

That's altered.
                            We lean to a cliff rail
Founded in tremblings.
Beneath us, two thousand five hundred
Miles of swung worldweight
Hit England's western wall
With a meaningless bump.

'Aye!' he sighs. Over and over. 'Aye!'
And massages his temples.

Can he grasp what's happened? His frown
Won't connect. Familiar eagle frown –
Dark imperial eye. The ground flinches.
Mountains of dissolution
Boil cold geysers, bespatter us.
                            Tranquillizers,
Steroids, and a whole crateful
Of escapist Madeira, collided
Three evenings ago –

They swamped and drowned
The synapses, the breath-born spinnaker shells
Of consonants and vowels.
                 I found him
Trying to get up out of a chair,
Fish-eyed, and choking, clawing at air,
Dumbness like a bone stuck in his throat.
He's survived with a word – one last word.
A last mouthful. I listen.
And I almost hear a new baby's
Eyeless howl of outrage – sobered to 'Aye!'
Sighed slow. Like blessed breath. He breathes it.

I dare hardly look at him. I watch.
He'd crept into my care.
A cursed hulk of marriage, a full-rigged fortune
Cast his body, crusted like Job's,
Onto my threshold. Strange Dead Sea creature.
He crawled in his ruins, like Timon.
The Times Index was his morning torture.
Fairy gold of a family of dead leaves.
'Why?' he'd cried. 'Why can't I just die?'
His memory was so sharp – a potsherd.
He raked at his skin, whispering 'God! God!'
Nightly, a nurse eased his scales with ointment.

I've brought him out for air. And the cliffs. And there
The sea towards America – wide open.
Untrodden, glorious America!
Look, a Peregrine Falcon – they're rare!

Nothing will connect.
He peers down past his shoes
Into a tangle of horizons –

Black, tilted bedrock struggling up,
Mouthing disintegration.

Every weedy breath of the sea
Is another swell of overwhelming.
Meaningless. And a sigh. Meaningless.

Now he's closed his eyes. He caresses
His own skull, over and over, comforting.
The Millmaster, the Caesar whose frown
Tossed my boyhood the baffling coin 'guilty'.
His fingers are my mother's. They seem astray
In quaverings and loss
As he strokes and strokes at his dome.
The sea thuds and sighs. Bowed at the rail
He seems to be touching at a wound he dare not touch.
He seems almost to find the exact spot.
His eyelids quiver, in the certainty of touch –

And 'Aye!' he breathes. 'Aye!'

We turn away. Then as he steadies himself,
Still gripping the rail, his reaching stare
Meets mine watching him. I can't escape it
Or hold it. Walt! Walt!
                              I bury it
Hugger-mugger anyhow
Inside my shirt.

Little Whale Song

for Charles Causley

What do they think of themselves
With their global brains –
The tide-power voltage illumination
Of those brains? Their X-ray all-dimension

Grasp of this world's structures, their brains budded
Clone replicas of the electron world

Lit and re-imagining the world,
Perfectly tuned receivers and perceivers,

Each one a whole tremulous world
Feeling through the world? What
Do they make of each other?

'We are beautiful. We stir

Our self-colour in the pot of colours
Which is the world. At each
Tail-stroke we deepen
Our being into the world's lit substance,

And our joy into the world's
Spinning bliss, and our peace
Into the world's floating, plumed peace.'

Their body-tons, echo-chambered,

Amplify the whisper
Of currents and airs, of sea-peoples

And planetary manoeuvres,
Of seasons, of shores, and of their own

Moon-lifted incantation, as they dance
Through the original Earth-drama
In which they perform, as from the beginning,
The Royal House.
                    The loftiest, spermiest

Passions, the most exquisite pleasures,
The noblest characters, the most god-like
Oceanic presence and poise –

The most terrible fall.

On the Reservations

for Jack Brown

I SITTING BULL ON CHRISTMAS MORNING

Who put this pit-head wheel,
Smashed but carefully folded
In some sooty fields, into his stocking?
And his lifetime nightshift – a snarl
Of sprung celluloid? Here's his tin flattened,
His helmet. And the actual sun closed
Into what looks like a bible of coal
That drops to bits as he lifts it. Very strange.
Packed in mossy woods, mostly ashes,
Here's a doll's cot. And a tiny coffin.

And here are Orca Tiger Eagle tattered
In his second birthday's ragbook
From before memory began.
All the props crushed, the ceilings collapsed
In his stocking. Torremolinos, Cleethorpes –
The brochures screwed up in a tantrum
As her hair shrivelled to a cinder
In his stocking. Pit boots. And, strange,
A London, burst, spewing tea-leaves,
With a creased postcard of the Acropolis.

Chapels pews broken television.
(Who dumped these, into his stocking,
Under coal-slag in a flooded cellar?)
Pink Uns and a million whippet collars –
Did he ask for these? A jumbo jet
Parcelled in starred, split, patched Christmas wrappings
Of a concrete yard and a brick wall
Black with scribble
In his stocking. No tobacco. A few
Rabbits and foxes broken leaking feathers.

Nevertheless, he feels like a new man –

Though tribally scarred (stitch-tattoos of coal-dust),
Though pale (soiled, the ivory bulb of a snowdrop
Dug up and tossed aside),
Though one of the lads (the horde, the spores of
  nowhere
Cultured under lamps and multiplied
In the laboratories
Between Mersey and Humber),
He stands, lungs easy, freed hands –
Bombarded by pollens from the supernovae,
Two eyepits awash in the millennia –

With his foot in his stocking.

II NIGHTVOICE

'My young men shall never work. Men who work cannot dream, and
wisdom comes in dreams.' *Smohalla, Nez Percé Indians*

She dreams she sleepwalks crying the Don River
relieves its nine
circles through her kitchen her kids
mops and brooms herself a squeegee and not
soaking in but
bulging pulsing out of their pores the
ordure *déjà vu* in Tesco's makes her
giddy

She dreams she sleepwalks crying her Dad alive
dug up is being
pushed into a wood-burning stove
by pensioners who chorus in croaks
While Shepherds
Watched Their television gives her
palpitations

She dreams she sleepwalks crying all the dead
huddle
in the slag-heaps wrong
land wrong
time tepees a final
resting for the epidemic
solution every
pit-shaft a
mass-grave herself
in a silly bottle shawled
in the canal's
fluorescence the message
of the survivors   a surplus people
the words
washed off her wrists
and hands she complains keep feeling
helpless

She dreams she sleepwalks mainstreet nightly crying
Stalin
keeps her as an ant
in a formicary in a
garbage-can which is his private office
urinal she thinks her aerials
must be bent

Remembering how a flare of pure torrent
sluiced the pit muck
off his shoulder-slopes while her hands
soapy with milk blossom anointed
him and in their hearth
fingers of the original sun opened
the black
bright book of the stone
he'd brought from beneath dreams
or did she dream it

III THE GHOST DANCER

'We are not singing sportive songs. It is as if we were weeping,
asking for life –' *Owl, Fox Indians*

A sulky boy. And he stuns your ear with song.
Swastika limbs, his whole physique – a dance.
The fool of prophecy, nightlong, daylong
Out of a waste lot brings deliverance.

Just some kid, with a demonic roar
Spinning *in vacuo*, inches clear of the floor.

Half-anguish half-joy, half-shriek half-moan:
He is the gorgon against his own fear.
Through his septum a dog's penile bone.
A chime of Chubb keys dangling at each ear.

Temenos Jaguar mask – a vogue mandala:
Half a Loa, half a drugged Oglala.

With woad cobras coiling their arm-clasp
Out of his each arm-pit, their ganch his grasp.

Bracelets, anklets; girlish, a bacchus chained.
An escapologist's pavement, padlock dance.
A mannequin elf, topped with a sugarfloss mane
Or neon rhino power-cone on a shorn sconce,

Or crest of a Cock of the Rock, or Cockatoo shock,
Or the sequinned crown of a Peacock.

And snake-spined, all pentecostal shivers,
This megawatt, berserker medium
With his strobe-drenched battle cry delivers
The nineteenth century from his mother's womb:

The work-house dread that brooded, through her term,
Over the despair of salvaged sperm.

Mau-Mau Messiah's showbiz lightning stroke
Puffs the stump of Empire up in smoke.

283

Brain-box back to front, heart inside out,
Aura for body, and for so-called soul
Under the moment's touch a reed that utters
Out of the solar cobalt core a howl

Bomblit, rainbowed, aboriginal:
'Start afresh, this time unconquerable.'

Rain-Charm for the Duchy

for H.R.H. Prince Harry

After the five-month drought
My windscreen was frosted with dust.
Sight itself had grown a harsh membrane
Against glare and particles.

Now the first blobby tears broke painfully.

Big, sudden thunderdrops. I felt them sploshing like
    vapoury petrol
Among the ants
In Cranmere's cracked heath-tinder. And into the ulcer
    craters
Of what had been river pools.

Then, like taking a great breath, we were under it.
Thunder gripped and picked up the city.
Rain didn't so much fall as collapse.
The pavements danced, like cinders in a riddle.

Flash in the pan, I thought, as people scampered.
Soon it was falling vertical, precious, pearled.
Thunder was a brass-band accompaniment
To some festive, civic event. Squeals and hurry. With
    tourist bunting.

The precinct saplings lifted their arms and faces. And the
    heaped-up sky
Moved in mayoral pomp, behind buildings,
With flash and thump. It had almost gone by
And I almost expected the brightening. Instead,
    something like a shutter

Jerked and rattled – and the whole county darkened.
Then rain really came down. You scrambled into the car
Scattering oxygen like a drenched bush.
What a weight of warm Atlantic water!

The car-top hammered. The Cathedral jumped in and out
Of a heaven that had obviously caught fire
And couldn't be contained.
A girl in high heels, her handbag above her head,

Risked it across the square's lit metals.
We saw surf cuffed over her and the car jounced.
Grates, gutters, clawed in the backwash.
She kept going. Flak and shrapnel

Of thundercracks
Hit the walls and roofs. Still a swimmer
She bobbed off, into sea-smoke,
Where headlights groped. Already

Thunder was breaking up the moors.
It dragged tors over the city –
Uprooted chunks of map. Smeltings of ore, pink and
    violet,
Spattered and wriggled down

Into the boiling sea
Where Exeter huddled –
A small trawler, nets out.
'Think of the barley!' you said.

You remembered earlier harvests.
But I was thinking
Of joyful sobbings –
The throb

In the rock-face mosses of the Chains,
And of the exultant larvae in the Barle's shrunk trench,
    their filaments ablur like propellers, under the churned
    ceiling of light,

And of the Lyn's twin gorges, clearing their throats,
    deepening their voices, beginning to hear each other
Rehearse forgotten riffles,

And the Mole, a ditch's choked whisper
Rousing the stagnant camps of the Little Silver, the
    Crooked Oak and the Yeo
To a commotion of shouts, muddied oxen
A rumbling of wagons,

And the red seepage, the smoke of life
Lowering its ringlets into the Taw,

And the Torridge, rising to the kiss,
Plunging under sprays, new-born,
A washed cherub, clasping the breasts of light,

And the Okement, nudging her detergent bottles,
    tugging at her nylon stockings, starting to trundle her
    Pepsi-Cola cans,

And the Tamar, roused and blinking under the fifty-mile
    drumming,
Declaiming her legend – her rusty knights tumbling out
    of their clay vaults, her cantrevs assembling from
    shillets,
With a cheering of aged stones along the Lyd and the
    Lew, the Wolf and the Thrushel,

And the Tavy, jarred from her quartzy rock-heap, feeling
    the moor shift
Rinsing her stale mouth, tasting tin, copper, ozone,

And the baby Erme, under the cyclone's top-heavy,
    toppling sea-fight, setting afloat odd bits of dead stick,

And the Dart, her shaggy horde coming down
Astride bareback ponies, with a cry,
Loosening sheepskin banners, bumping the granite,
Flattening rowans and frightening oaks,

And the Teign, startled in her den
By the rain-dance of bracken
Hearing Heaven reverberate under Gidleigh,

And the highest pool of the Exe, her coil recoiling under
  the sky-shock
Where a drinking stag flings its head up
From a spilled skyful of lightning –

My windscreen wipers swam as we moved.
                                  I imagined the two moors
The two stone-age hands
Cupped and brimming, lifted, an offering –
And I thought of those other, different lightnings, the
  patient, thirsting ones

Under Crow Island, inside Bideford Bar,
And between the Hamoaze anchor chains,
And beneath the thousand, shivering, fibreglass hulls
Inside One Gun Point, and aligned

Under the Ness, and inside Great Bull Hill:

The salmon, deep in the thunder, lit
And again lit, with glimpses of quenchings,
Twisting their glints in the suspense,
Biting at the stir, beginning to move.

Old Oats

'Mad Laughter', your sister – her grey perm
Rayed out in electrified frazzles.
But you were the backfiring
Heart of your double-humped,
Sooty, two hundred acres.
Alex cracked. Strabismic, pitiable,
Gawky, adopted Alex!
That morning on the stack – and you
In a Führer frenzy,
Your coalface vocabulary
Going up in one flame!
Alex never came back.
Where did you end up?
Chimpanzee, dangle-pawed,
Shambling, midget ogre. Jehovah
Of my fallen Eden.
Undershot, bristly jowl –
Chimpanzee. That dazzled scowl –
Chimpanzee. Shoulder wing-stumps
In the waistcoat bossed
And polished to metal –
Chimpanzee. Cap an oil-rag,
Chewing your twist,
Raw disintegrating boots –
Your free knuckles lay quaking
At ease on the mudguard
Or pointed out to me
The bright, startling, pretty
Shrapnel in the stubble.
Your spittle curse, bitten off

Among the unshaven silver,
You'd give me the damned farm!
Nothing too stubborn,
Ferguson brains, running on pink paraffin,
Up in the dark, head in the cow's crutch
Under the throb of Dorniers,
Staring into the warm foam,
Hobbling with a bucket and a lantern
Under the sky-burn of Sheffield,
Breaking your labourers with voice –
A royal succession of Georges!
What was it all for?
Collapsing between the stooks,
Up again, jump-starting your old engine
With your hip-flask,
Hoisting the top-heavy stackyard
Summer after summer. How many horses
Worn to chaffy dust? How many tractors
Battered to scrap? What's become of you? Nobody
Could have kept it up. Only
One thing's certain. Somewhere
You rest.

The Last of the 1st/5th Lancashire Fusiliers

A Souvenir of the Gallipoli Landings

The father capers across the yard cobbles
Look, like a bird, a water-bird, an ibis going over pebbles
We laughed, like warships fluttering bunting.

Heavy-duty design, deep-seated in ocean-water
The warships flutter bunting.
A fiesta day for the warships
Where war is only an idea, as drowning is only an idea
In the folding of a wave, in the mourning

Funeral procession, the broadening wake
That follows a ship under power.

War is an idea in the muzzled calibre of the big guns.
In the grey, wolvish outline.
War is a kind of careless health, like the heart-beat
In the easy bodies of sailors, feeling the big engines
Idling between emergencies.

It is what has left the father
Who has become a bird.
Once he held war in his strong pint mugful of tea
And drank at it, heavily sugared.
It was all for him
Under the parapet, under the periscope, the look-out
Under Achi Baba and the fifty billion flies.

Now he has become a long-billed, spider-kneed bird
Bow-backed, finding his footing, over the frosty cobbles
A wader, picking curiosities from the shallows.

His sons don't know why they laughed, watching him
    through the window
Remembering it, remembering their laughter
They only want to weep

As after the huge wars

Senseless huge wars

Huge senseless weeping.

Anniversary

My mother in her feathers of flame
Grows taller. Every May Thirteenth
I see her with her sister Miriam. I lift
The torn-off diary page where my brother jotted
'Ma died today' – and there they are.

She is now as tall as Miriam.
In the perpetual Sunday morning
Of everlasting, they are strolling together
Listening to the larks
Ringing in their orbits. The work of the cosmos,
Creation and destruction of matter
And of anti-matter
Pulses and flares, shudders and fades
Like the Northern Lights in their feathers.

My mother is telling Miriam
About her life, which was mine. Her voice comes, piping,
Down a deep gorge of woodland echoes:
'This is the water-line, dark on my dress, look,
Where I dragged him from the reservoir.
And that is the horse on which I galloped
Through the brick wall
And out over the heather simply
To bring him a new pen. This is the pen
I laid on the altar. And these
Are the mass marriages of him and his brother
Where I was not once a guest.' Then suddenly
She is scattering the red coals with her fingers
To find where I had fallen
For the third time. She laughs
Helplessly till she weeps. Miriam
Who died at eighteen
Is Madonna-like with pure wonder
To hear of all she missed. Now my mother
Shows her the rosary prayers of unending worry,
Like pairs of shoes, or one dress after another,
'This is the sort of thing,' she is saying,
'I liked to wear best.' And: 'Much of it,
You know, was simply sitting at the window
Watching the horizon. Truly
Wonderful it was, day after day,

Knowing they were somewhere. It still is.
Look.'

And they pause, on the brink
Of the starry dew. They are looking at me.
My mother, darker with her life,
Her Red Indian hair, her skin
So strangely olive and other-worldly,
Miriam now sheer flame beside her.
Their feathers throb softly, iridescent.
My mother's face is glistening
As if she held it into the skyline wind
Looking towards me. I do this for her.

She is using me to tune finer
Her weeping love for my brother, through mine,
As if I were the shadow cast by his approach.

As when I came a mile over fields and walls
Towards her, and found her weeping for him –
Able for all that distance to think me him.

Chaucer

'Whan that Aprille with his shoures soote
The droghte of March hath perced to the roote . . .'
At the top of your voice, where you swayed on the top of
    a stile,
Your arms raised – somewhat for balance, somewhat
To hold the reins of the straining attention
Of your imagined audience – you declaimed Chaucer
To a field of cows. And the Spring sky had done it
With its flying laundry, and the new emerald
Of the thorns, the hawthorn, the blackthorn,
And one of those bumpers of champagne
You snatched unpredictably from pure spirit.

Your voice went over the fields towards Grantchester.
It must have sounded lost. But the cows
Watched, then approached: they appreciated Chaucer.
You went on and on. Here were reasons
To recite Chaucer. Then came the Wyf of Bath,
Your favourite character in all literature.
You were rapt. And the cows were enthralled.
They shoved and jostled shoulders, making a ring,
To gaze into your face, with occasional snorts
Of exclamation, renewed their astounded attention,
Ears angling to catch every inflection,
Keeping their awed six feet of reverence
Away from you. You just could not believe it.
And you could not stop. What would happen
If you were to stop? Would they attack you,
Scared by the shock of silence, or wanting more – ?
So you had to go on. You went on –
And twenty cows stayed with you hypnotized.
How did you stop? I can't remember
You stopping. I imagine they reeled away –
Rolling eyes, as if driven from their fodder.
I imagine I shooed them away. But
Your sostenuto rendering of Chaucer
Was already perpetual. What followed
Found my attention too full
And had to go back into oblivion.

You Hated Spain

                    Spain frightened you. Spain
Where I felt at home. The blood-raw light,
The oiled anchovy faces, the African
Black edges to everything, frightened you.
Your schooling had somehow neglected Spain.
The wrought-iron grille, death and the Arab drum.

You did not know the language, your soul was empty
Of the signs, and the welding light
Made your blood shrivel. Bosch
Held out a spidery hand and you took it
Timidly, a bobby-sox American.
You saw right down to the Goya funeral grin
And recognized it, and recoiled
As your poems winced into chill, as your panic
Clutched back towards college America.
So we sat as tourists at the bullfight
Watching bewildered bulls awkwardly butchered,
Seeing the grey-faced matador, at the barrier
Just below us, straightening his bent sword
And vomiting with fear. And the horn
That hid itself inside the blowfly belly
Of the toppled picador punctured
What was waiting for you. Spain
Was the land of your dreams: the dust-red cadaver
You dared not wake with, the puckering amputations
No literature course had glamorized.
The juju land behind your African lips.
Spain was what you tried to wake up from
And could not. I see you, in moonlight,
Walking the empty wharf at Alicante
Like a soul waiting for the ferry,
A new soul, still not understanding,
Thinking it is still your honeymoon
In the happy world, with your whole life waiting,
Happy, and all your poems still to be found.

The Earthenware Head

Who modelled your head of terracotta?
Some American student friend.
Life-size, the lips half-pursed, raw-edged

With crusty tooling – a naturalistic attempt
At a likeness that just failed. You did not like it.
I did not like it. Unease magnetized it
For a perverse rite. What possessed us
To take it with us, in your red bucket bag?
November fendamp haze, the river unfurling
Dark whorls, ferrying slender willow yellows.
The pollard willows wore comfortless antlers,
Switch-horns, leafless. Just past where the field
Broadens and the path strays up to the right
To lose the river and puzzle for Grantchester,
A chosen willow leaned towards the water.
Above head height, the socket of a healed bole-wound,
A twiggy crotch, nearly an owl's porch,
Made a mythic shrine for your double.
I fitted it upright, firm. And a willow tree
Was a Herm, with your head, watching East
Through those tool-stabbed pupils. We left it
To live the world's life and weather forever.

You ransacked Thesaurus in your poem about it,
Veiling its mirror, rhyming yourself into safety
From its orphaned fate.
But it would not leave you. Weeks later
We could not seem to hit on the tree. We did not
Look too hard – just in passing. Already
You did not want to fear, if it had gone,
What witchcraft might ponder it. You never
Said much more about it.
                                    What happened?
Maybe nothing happened. Perhaps
It is still there, representing you
To the sunrise, and happy
In its cold pastoral, lips pursed slightly
As if my touch had only just left it.
Or did boys find it – and shatter it? Or
Did the tree too kneel finally?

Surely the river got it. Surely
The river is its chapel. And keeps it. Surely
Your deathless head, fired in a furnace,
Face to face at last, kisses the Father
Mudded at the bottom of the Cam,
Beyond recognition or rescue,
All our fears washed from it, and perfect,
Under the stained mournful flow, saluted
Only in summer briefly by the slender
Punt-loads of shadows flitting towards their honey
And the stopped clock.
                          Evil.
That was what you called the head. Evil.

The Tender Place

Your temples, where the hair crowded in,
Were the tender place. Once to check
I dropped a file across the electrodes
Of a twelve-volt battery – it exploded
Like a grenade. Somebody wired you up.
Somebody pushed the lever. They crashed
The thunderbolt into your skull.
In their bleached coats, with blenched faces,
They hovered again
To see how you were, in your straps.
Whether your teeth were still whole.
The hand on the calibrated lever
Again feeling nothing
Except feeling nothing pushed to feel
Some squirm of sensation. Terror
Was the cloud of you
Waiting for these lightnings. I saw
An oak limb sheared at a bang.
You your Daddy's leg. How many seizures

Did you suffer this god to grab you
By the roots of the hair? The reports
Escaped back into clouds. What went up
Vaporized? Where lightning rods wept copper
And the nerve threw off its skin
Like a burning child
Scampering out of the bomb-flash. They dropped you
A rigid bent bit of wire
Across the Boston City grid. The lights
In the Senate House dipped
As your voice dived inwards

Right through the bolt-hole basement.
Came up, years later,
Over-exposed, like an X-ray –
Brain-map still dark-patched
With the scorched-earth scars
Of your retreat. And your words,
Faces reversed from the light,
Holding in their entrails.

Black Coat

I remember going out there,
The tide far out, the North Shore ice-wind
Cutting me back
To the quick of the blood – that outer-edge nostalgia,
The good feeling. My sole memory
Of my black overcoat. Padding the wet sandspit.
I was staring at the sea, I suppose.
Trying to feel thoroughly alone,
Simply myself, with sharp edges –
Me and the sea one big tabula rasa,
As if my returning footprints
Out of that scrim of gleam, that horizon-wide wipe,
Might be a whole new start.

My shoe-sole shapes
My only sign.
My minimal but satisfying discussion
With the sea.
Putting my remarks down, for the thin tongue
Of the sea to interpret. Inaudibly.
A therapy,
Instructions too complicated for me
At the moment, but stowed in my black box for later.
Like feeding a wild deer
With potato crisps
As you do in that snapshot where you exclaim
Back towards me and my camera.

So I had no idea I had stepped
Into the telescopic sights
Of the paparazzo sniper
Nested in your brown iris.
Perhaps you had no idea either,
So far off, half a mile maybe,
Looking towards me. Watching me
Pin the sea's edge down.
No idea
How that double image,
Your eye's inbuilt double exposure
Which was the projection
Of your two-way heart's diplopic error,
The body of the ghost and me the blurred see-through
Came into single focus,
Sharp-edged, stark as a target,
Set up like a decoy
Against that freezing sea
From which your dead father had just crawled.

I did not feel
How, as your lenses tightened,
He slid into me.

Being Christlike

You did not want to be Christlike. Though your Father
Was your God and there was no other, you did not
Want to be Christlike. Though you walked
In the love of your Father. Though you stared
At the stranger your Mother.
What had she to do with you
But tempt you from your Father?
When her great hooded eyes lowered
Their moon so close
Promising the earth you saw
Your fate and you cried
Get thee behind me. You did not
Want to be Christlike. You wanted
To be with your Father
In wherever he was. And your body
Barred your passage. And your family
Which were your flesh and blood
Burdened it. And a god
That was not your Father
Was a false god. But you did not
Want to be Christlike.

The God

You were like a religious fanatic
Without a god – unable to pray.
You wanted to be a writer.
Wanted to write? What was it within you
Had to tell its tale?
The story that has to be told
Is the writer's God, who calls
Out of sleep, inaudibly: 'Write.'
Write what?

Your heart, mid-Sahara, raged
In its emptiness.
Your dreams were empty.
You bowed at your desk and you wept
Over the story that refused to exist,
As over a prayer
That could not be prayed
To a non-existent God. A dead God
With a terrible voice.
You were like those desert ascetics
Who fascinated you,
Parching in such a torturing
Vacuum of God
It sucked goblins out of their finger-ends,
Out of the soft motes of the sun-shaft,
Out of the blank rock face.
The gagged prayer of their sterility
Was a God.
So was your panic of emptiness – a God.

You offered him verses. First
Little phials of the emptiness
Into which your panic dropped its tears
That dried and left crystalline spectra.
Crusts of salt from your sleep.
Like the dewy sweat
On some desert stones, after dawn.
Oblations to an absence.
Little sacrifices. Soon

Your silent howl through the night
Had made itself a moon, a fiery idol
Of your God.
Your crying carried its moon
Like a woman a dead child. Like a woman
Nursing a dead child, bending to cool
Its lips with tear-drops on her finger-tip,

301

So I nursed you, who nursed a moon
That was human but dead, withered and
Burned you like a lump of phosphorus.

Till the child stirred. Its mouth-hole stirred.
Blood oozed at your nipple,
A drip feed of blood. Our happy moment!

The little god flew up into the Elm Tree.
In your sleep, glassy eyed,
You heard its instructions. When you woke
Your hands moved. You watched them in dismay
As they made a new sacrifice.
Two handfuls of blood, your own blood,
And in that blood gobbets of me,
Wrapped in a tissue of story that had somehow
Slipped from you. An embryo story.
You could not explain it or who
Ate at your hands.
The little god roared at night in the orchard,
His roar half a laugh.

You fed him by day, under your hair-tent,
Over your desk, in your secret
Spirit house, you whispered,
You drummed on your thumb with your fingers,
Shook Winthrop shells for their sea-voices,
And gave me an effigy – a Salvia
Pressed in a Lutheran Bible.
You could not explain it. Sleep had opened.
Darkness poured from it, like perfume.
Your dreams had burst their coffin.
Blinded I struck a light

And woke upside down in your spirit-house
Moving limbs that were not my limbs,
And telling, in a voice not my voice,
A story of which I knew nothing,

Giddy
With the smoke of the fire you tended
Flames I had lit unwitting
That whitened in the oxygen jet
Of your incantatory whisper.

You fed the flames with the myrrh of your mother
The frankincense of your father
And your own amber and the tongues
Of fire told their tale. And suddenly
Everybody knew everything.
Your God snuffed up the fatty reek.
His roar was like a basement furnace
In your ears, thunder in the foundations.

Then you wrote in a fury, weeping,
Your joy a trance-dancer
In the smoke in the flames.
'God is speaking through me,' you told me.
'Don't say that,' I cried, 'Don't say that.
That is horribly unlucky!'
As I sat there with blistering eyes
Watching everything go up
In the flames of your sacrifice
That finally caught you too till you
Vanished, exploding
Into the flames
Of the story of your God
Who embraced you
And your mummy and your daddy –
Your Aztec, Black Forest
God of the euphemism Grief.

The Dogs Are Eating Your Mother

That is not your mother but her body.
She leaped from our window
And fell there. Those are not dogs
That seem to be dogs
Pulling at her. Remember the lean hound
Running up the lane holding high
The dangling raw windpipe and lungs
Of a fox? Now see who
Will drop on all fours at the end of the street
And come romping towards your mother,
Pulling her remains, with their lips
Lifted like dog's lips
Into new positions. Protect her
And they will tear you down
As if you were more her.
They will find you every bit
As succulent as she is. Too late
To salvage what she was.
I buried her where she fell.
You played around the grave. We arranged
Sea-shells and big veined pebbles
Carried from Appledore
As if we were herself. But a kind
Of hyena came aching upwind.
They dug her out. Now they batten
On the cornucopia
Of her body. Even
Bite the face off her gravestone,
Gulp down the grave ornaments,
Swallow the very soil.
                              So leave her.
Let her be their spoils. Go wrap
Your head in the snowy rivers
Of the Brooks Range. Cover

Your eyes with the writhing airs
Off the Nullarbor Plains. Let them
Jerk their tail-stumps, bristle and vomit
Over their symposia.
                    Think her better
Spread with holy care on a high grid
For vultures
To take back into the sun. Imagine
These bone-crushing mouths the mouths
That labour for the beetle
Who will roll her back into the sun.

The Other

She had too much so with a smile you took some.
Of everything she had you had
Absolutely nothing, so you took some.
At first, just a little.

Still she had so much she made you feel
Your vacuum, which nature abhorred,
So you took your fill, for nature's sake.
Because her great luck made you feel unlucky
You had redressed the balance, which meant
Now you had some too, for yourself.
As seemed only fair. Still her ambition
Claimed the natural right to screw you up
Like a crossed-out page, tossed into a basket.
Somebody, on behalf of the gods,
Had to correct that hubris.
A little touch of hatred steadied the nerves.

Everything she had won, the happiness of it,
You collected
As your compensation
For having lost. Which left her absolutely

Nothing. Even her life was
Trapped in the heap you took. She had nothing.
Too late you saw what had happened.
It made no difference that she was dead.
Now that you had all she had ever had
You had much too much.
                                        Only you
Saw her smile, as she took some.
At first, just a little.

The Locket

Sleeping and waking in the Song of Songs
You were half-blissful. But on occasion
Casually as a yawn, you'd open
Your death and contemplate it.

Your death
Was so utterly within your power
It was as if you had trapped it. Maybe by somehow
Giving it some part of you, for its food.
Now it was your curio pet,
Your familiar. But who else would have nursed it
In a locket between her breasts!

Smiling, you'd hold it up.
You'd swing it on its chain, to tease life.
It lent you uncanny power. A secret, blueish,
Demonic flash
When you smiled and gently bit the locket.

I have read how a fiery cross
Can grow and brighten in the dreams of a spinster.
But a crooked key turned in your locket.
It had sealed your door in Berlin
With the brand of the burnt. You knew exactly

How your death looked. It was a long-cold oven
Locked with a swastika.

The locket kept splitting open.
I would close it. You would smile.
Its lips kept coming apart – just a slit.
The clasp seemed to be faulty.
Who could have guessed what it was trying to say?
Your beauty, a folktale wager,
Was a quarter century posthumous.

While I juggled our futures, it kept up its whisper
To my deafened ear: *fait accompli*.

Shibboleth

Your German
Found its royal licence in the English
Your mother had bought (peering into the future)
By mail order, from Fortnum and Mason. Your Hebrew
Survived on bats and spiders
In the guerrilla priest-hole
Under your tongue. Nevertheless,
At the long-weekend Berkshire county table,
In a dizzy silence, your cheekbones
(From the Black Sea, where the roses bloom thrice)
Flushed sootier –
Stared at by English hounds
Whose tails had stopped wagging. When the lips lifted,
The trade-routes of the Altai
Tangled in your panic, tripped you. It was
The frontier glare of customs.
The gun-barrels
Of the imperious noses
Pointed at something pinioned. Then a drawl:
'Lick of the tar-brush?'

There you saw it,
Your lonely Tartar death,
Surrounded and 'dumb like the bound
Wolf on Tolstoy's horse'.

Snow

Snow falling. Snowflakes clung and melted
In the sparkly black fox fur of your hat.
Soft chandeliers, ghostly wreckage
Of the Moscow Opera. Flakes perching and
Losing their hold on the heather tips. An unending
Walk down the cobbled hill into the oven
Of empty fire. Among the falling
Heavens. A short walk
That could never end was
Never ending. Down, on down
Under the thick, loose flocculence
Of a life
Burning out in the air. Between char-black buildings
Converted to closed cafés and Brontë gift-shops.
Beyond them, the constellations falling
Through the Judaean thorns, into the fleeces
Of the Pennine sheep. Deepening
Over the faces of your school-friends,
Beside their snowed-under tanks, locked into the Steppe
Where the mud had frozen again
While they drank their coffee. You escaped
Deeper into the falling flakes. They were clinging
To the charcoal crimped black ponyskin
Coat you wore. Words seemed warm. They
Melted in our mouths
Whatever was trying to cling.
                                   Leaning snow

Folded you under its cloak and ushered you away
Down the hill. Back to where you came from.

I watched you. Feeling the snow's touch.

Already, it was burying your footprints,
Drawing its white sheet over everything,
Closing the air behind you.

Folktale

He did not know she had risen out of cinders.
She knew he had nothing.
So they ransacked each other. What he wanted
Was the gold, black-lettered pelt
Of the leopard of Ein-Gedi.
She wanted only the runaway slave.
What he wanted was Turgenev's antimacassar.
She wanted escape without a passport.
What he wanted was Bach's aerobatic
Gutturals in Arabic.
She wanted the enemy without his gun.
He wanted the seven treasures of Asia –
Skin, eyes, lips, blood, hair knotted roughly
In seven different flags.
She wanted the silent heraldry
Of the purple beech by the noble wall.
He wanted Cabala the ghetto demon
With its polythene bag full of ashes.
She wanted only shade from the noon's
Broken-armed Catherine Wheel
Under an island leaf. She wanted
A love-knot Eden-cool as two lob-worms
And a child of acorn.
He wanted a mother of halva.
She wanted the hill-stream's tabula rasa.

He wanted the thread-end of himself.
So they ransacked each other for everything
That could not be found. And their fingers met
And were wrestling, like flames
In the crackling thorns
Of everything they lacked –

                              as midnight struck.

Opus 131

Opus 131 in C Sharp Minor
Opened the great door
In the air, and through it
Flooded horror. The door in the hotel room
And the curtain at the window and even
The plain homely daylight blocking the window
Were in the wrong dimension
To shut it out. The counterpoint pinned back
The flaps of the body. Naked, faceless,
The heart panted there, like a foetus.
Where was the lifeline music? What had happened
To consolation, prayer, transcendence –
To the selective disconnecting
Of the pain centre? Dark insects
Fought with their instruments
Scampering through your open body
As if you had already left it. Beethoven
Had broken down. You strained listening
Maybe for divorce to be resolved
In the arithmetic of vibration
To pure zero, for the wave-particles
To pronounce on the unimportance
Of the menopause. Beethoven
Was trying to repair
The huge constellations of his silence

That flickered and glinted in the wind.
But the notes, with their sharp faces,
Were already carrying you off,
Each with a different bit, into the corners
Of the Universe.

Descent

You had to strip off Germany
The crisp shirt with its crossed lightnings
And go underground.
You were forced to strip off Israel
The bodice woven of the hairs of the cactus
To be bullet-proof, and go deeper.
You had to strip off Russia
With those ear-rings worn in honour
Of Eugene Onegin. And go deeper.
You had to strip off British Columbia
And the fish-skin mock-up waterproof
From the cannery, with its erotic motif
Of porcupine quills, that pierced you
And came with you, working deeper
As you moved deeper.
Finally you had to strip off England
With your wedding rings
And go deeper.
                    Then suddenly you were abandoned
By the gem-stones, rubies, emeralds, all you had
    hoarded
In a fold of paper
At the back of a drawer -- you had thought
These would protect you in the end,
Urim and Thummim. Cowardly
They scattered in the splinters of weeping
As your own hands, stronger than your choked outcry,

Took your daughter from you. She was stripped from
    you,
The last raiment
Clinging round your neck, the sole remnant
Between you and the bed
In the underworld
            Where Inanna
Has to lie naked, between strata
That can never be opened, except as a book.

The Error

When her grave opened its ugly mouth
Why didn't you just fly,
Wrap yourself in your hair and make yourself scarce,
Why did you kneel down at the grave's edge
To be identified
Accused and convicted
By all who held in their hands
Pieces of the gravestone grey granite
Proof of their innocence?

You must have misheard a sentence.
You were always mishearing
Into Hebrew or German
What was muttered in English.
Her grave mouthed its riddle right enough.
But maybe you heard in the air somewhere
An answer to one of your own
Unspoken enigmas. Misheard,
Mistook, and kneeled meekly.

Maybe they wouldn't stone you
If you became a nun
And selflessly incinerated yourself
In the shrine of her death.

Because that is what you did. From that moment
Shops, jobs, baby daughter, the German au pair
Had to become mere shapes
In the offered-up flames, a kind of writhing
That enfolded you and devoured
Your whole life.
I watched you feeding the flames.
Why didn't you wrap yourself in a carpet
Get to a hospital
Drop the whole mistake – simply call it
An error in translation?

Instead you fed those flames
Six full calendar years –
Every tarred and brimstone
Day torn carefully off,
One at a time, not one wasted, patient
As if you were feeding a child.
You were not feeding a child.
All you were doing was being strong,
Waiting for your ashes
To be complete and to cool.

Finally they made a small cairn.

Lines about Elias

for Thom Gunn

Did music help him? Indeed it helped him.
His crude music, instruments
Imitated uncannily but weirdly
Restored the order of music
Within the terror of the Camp.
They could have been baboons
In some demented phase of tribal breakdown

During a famine, or under the effects
Of a poisonous dust from space.
Yet his music, for its few moments
Ushered them into a formation
Where the Camp did not exist
Where their sorrowful bodies did not exist.

So the scabies on his belly the sores and
Inflammations which made Elias
That ferocious clown crow
And ridiculed him, ripping down his trousers
Fighting with him in the mud
They did not touch his music
Did not adhere to any note of it
Or disturb his performance
Through which his fellow-prisoners escaped
Their rags, their last few horrible hours, their next few
Frightful possibly fatal days, sooner
Or later nearly certainly fatal days
Standing aside from them, stepping a little
Out of the time corridor, standing in a group
Just outside it, where the air was still,

In the solidarity of souls, where music uttered
The dumbness of naked bodies
As if it were the inside of the earth
And everything else –
The hours where their soft surfaces
Tore against the hard –
Were merely rags
It happened to wear, and could ignore.

Music poured out of nowhere
Strange food
And made them for those moments unaware
Of their starvation and indifferent
To their humanity

While the guards too, shedding and
Escaping their humanity
Lowered themselves into the sound
As into a communal bath
Where all were anonymous new-born
Innocent all equally
Innocent equally defenceless

The guards indeed more defenceless
More terribly naked needing
The music more

A Dove

Snaps its twig-tether – mounts –
Dream-yanked up into vacuum
Wings snickering.

Another, in a shatter, hurls dodging away up.

They career through tree-mazes –
Nearly uncontrollable love-weights.

Or now
Temple-dancers, possessed, and steered
By solemn powers
Through insane, stately convulsions.

Porpoises
Of dove-lust and blood splendour
With arcs
And plungings, and spray-slow explosions.

Now violently gone
Riding the snake of the long love-whip
Among flarings of mares and stallions

Now staying
Coiled on a bough
Bubbling molten, wobbling top-heavy
Into one and many.

INDEXES

INDEX OF TITLES

INDEX OF FIRST LINES

Honeysuckle hanging her fangs 262
How it hung 211

I am the hunted king 103
I climbed through woods in the hour-before-dawn dark 7
I felt a strange fear when the war-talk 273
I flash-glimpsed in the headlights – the high moment 188
I found this jawbone at the sea's edge 29
I had exploded, a bombcloud, lop-headed, my huge fingers 53
I know well 153
I imagine this midnight moment's forest 3
In Hardcastle Crags, that echoey museum 158
In the beginning was Scream 90
In the dawn-dirty light, in the biggest snow of the year 181
In the huge, wide-open, sleeping eye of the mountain 64
I park the car half in the ditch and switch off and sit 45
I remember going out there 298
I see the oak's bride in the oak's grasp 150
I sit in the top of the wood, my eyes closed 29
Is melting an old frost moon 107
I stood on a dark summit, among dark summits 167
Is without world 84
I was just walking about 267
I whispered to the holly 50
I woke to a shout: 'I am Alpha and Omega' 70

Join water, wade in underbeing 255
Jumbled iceberg hills, away to the North 250
Just before the curtain falls in the river 260

Light words forsook them 165
Like a propped skull 49
Looking close in the evil mirror Crow saw 101

'Mad Laughter', your sister – her grey perm 289
Man's and woman's bodies lay without souls 91
Mid-May – after May frosts that killed the Camellias 223
My father sat in his chair recovering 72
My mother in her feathers of flame 291
My neighbour moves less and less, attempts less 63
My post-war father was so silent 269

new to the blood 206
No, the serpent did not 70

Where there was nothing 172
Who lived at the top end of our street 35
Who modelled your head of terracotta? 295
Who owns these scrawny little feet? *Death* 90
Who put this pit-head wheel 280
Who's killed the leaves? 142
Wind out of freezing Europe. A mean snow 178

Yesterday he was nowhere to be found 235
You did not want to be Christlike. Though your Father 300
You had to strip off Germany 311
Your hosts are almost glad he gate-crashed: see 11
Your bony white bowed back, in a singlet 191
Your German 307
Your temples, where the hair crowded in 297
Your tree – your oak 155
You were like a religious fanatic 300